Practical Project Management
from Strategy to Realization

Abi Akindele

Practical Project Management
from Strategy to Realization

Abi Akindele, MBA, PMP

First Edition: August, 2009 (*black & white printing*)

Published by:

SaturnBay Corporation, Toronto, Canada
Website: www.saturnbay.ca
Email: support@saturnbay.ca

Printed in the United States of America.

ISBN: 1448693837
EAN-13: 9781448693832

Abbey

Dedication

I dedicate this book to those who have shown courage, sought and applied knowledge and wisdom for the good of mankind, even in the face of adversity.

Acknowledgements

This book would not have been completed to this level of clarity and professionalism without the committed effort of professional colleagues, friends and well-wishers. I will like to express my sincere and profound appreciation to the following people of substance, for their commendable contributions and support to making this book a reality: Ramez Habibzadeh, Khalidah Bello, Julius Kolawole, Harp Ahluwalia, Anissa Rahim, TK Olatinwo, Kunle Oladebo and Fan Cheng. They have more than 150 years of experience from different industries - oil & gas, finance, information technology & management, government, services and research & development.

Special thanks to Ramez, Julius, Kunle and TK for their diligent reviews of the book from cover to cover and vital feedback that enhanced the quality of the book. I also thank the following friends and well-wishers for their moral support: Vincent Asor, Toyosi Bello and Raphael Olabisi.

In conclusion, I am thankful to God (the Spirit of the truth) for giving me the opportunity and energy to commit myself to sharing of knowledge through writing, which I enjoyed so much and has contributed significantly to my personal fulfillment.

Table of Content

Table of Figures

List of Templates

Part 1: Agenda

This part set the stage for this book. It includes the following:

- Mission and Scope
- Theme
- Book Summary, Update and Legend
- Target Audience
- Caution - What you will get

Blank page

Chapter 1 - Mission and Scope

"Everything should be made as simple as possible, but not simpler."   *Albert Einstein*

Mission

The mission of this book is to create a practical real life guide that facilitates effective management and successful delivery of projects of all sizes and goal oriented activities, at all times.

Scope

This book provides a clear path on how to navigate from strategy to project delivery (realization). Its focus is on what and how of effective project management. It describes the generic and practical processes, deliverables, people, techniques and tools and, most importantly, good practices for project and business management professionals, business managers and executives.

This book complements standard industry project and business management methodologies. It provides guidance on how to navigate from strategy to portfolio management and project management. Its focus is not on strategy development and portfolio management. It is presented in a consistent style that enables the user to effectively use and adapt the practical processes, techniques, tools and good practices to successfully manage projects.

Most of the approaches, processes, techniques, tools and good practices in this book are those that I have used practically to successfully deliver projects of different sizes. I believe you will find them useful, adaptable and effective for managing and delivering your projects.

This book is guaranteed to be filled with substance and no fluffy stuff. All statements, charts and templates have been carefully constructed and presented to make practical sense to the reader. The contents were written based on extensive research, personal knowledge and experience, which make the book realistic and practically useful. References were made to industry practices and knowledge base to ensure consistency and complementary presentation. The sequence of the presentation provides a good understanding of project management practices within the context of the overall organization's business framework.

The term "good practices" is used in this book, instead of "best practices". I do not want to assume that the suggested practices are the only way to get things done, rather as preferred and well tested practices which have yielded quality results. Also, alternatives or better practices emerge all the time and I do not want the reader to lose sight of that.

Theme

Deliver projects successfully at all times

If you cannot imagine it, that is seeing a clear path from the start to the end, do not commit to it. You should always have the end in mind as your driver for success. Move from imagination to envisioning, to architecture/design, to development and to realization.

Project management is about planning, managing and implementing an endeavour, with a clearly defined outcome. The desired outcome should be clearly defined before the project is initiated. Besides research, excluded from this discussion, it is rare for anyone to commit to or pay for an unknown outcome. An event without a clear definition of the outcome could be considered as a gamble.

A project may be stopped or canceled due to legitimate reasons, particularly those that are outside the control of the project. For instance, a project may be stopped because of a product in development whose latest value assessment could no longer deliver a real commercial value. The goal is to ensure that, within the project control, projects are managed and delivered successfully, external or exogenous factors permitting. Most projects that failed are because some people, most often, fail to learn before, during and after the event. Cooperative effort of the stakeholders, consistent application of practical methods, techniques, tools and good practices facilitate all-time successful delivery of projects.

Chapter 2 - Book Summary

The outline of this book is shown in Figure 1.

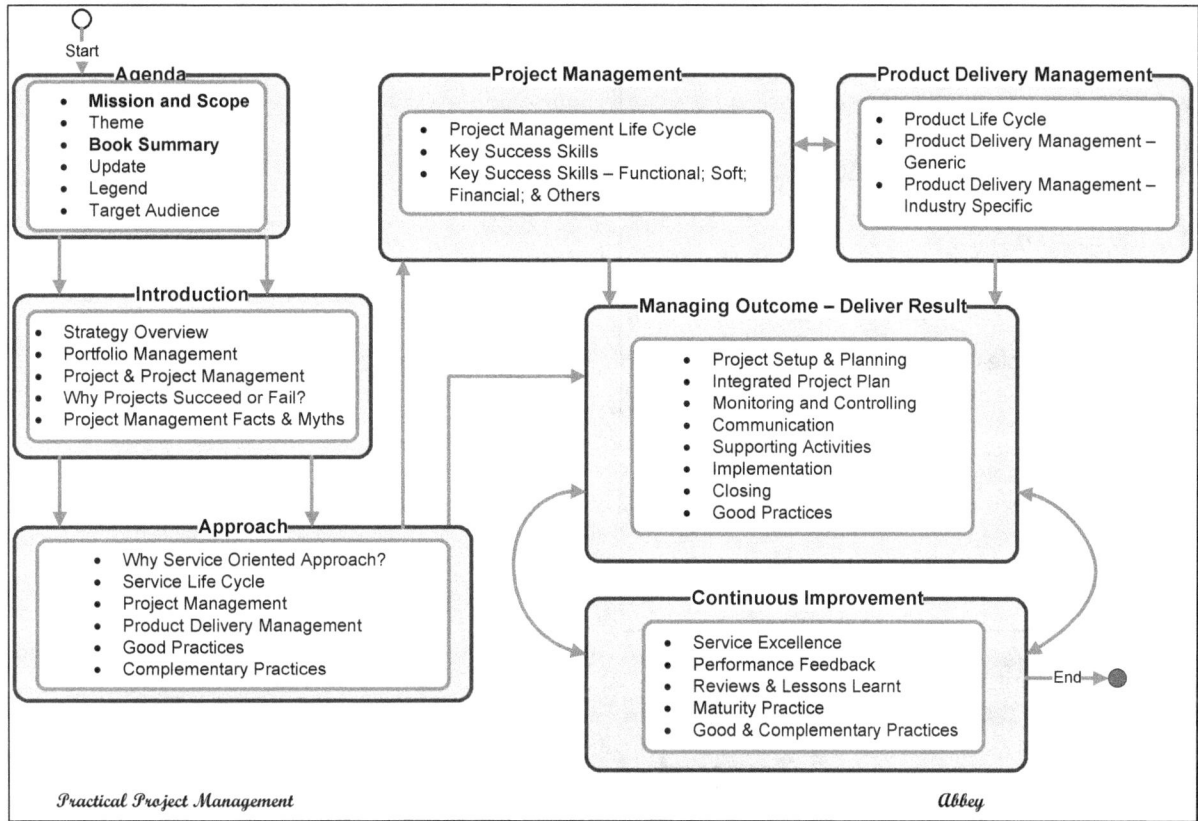

Figure 1 - Agenda, Book Outline

Update

This book will be updated regularly to include good practices, improved presentations, refined techniques, tools and templates to aid successful delivery of projects. It will be available in both printed and electronic formats. The electronic or eBook format will include all the templates and facilitate highly accessible, fastest and up-to-date product delivery. For the printed format, the eBook and templates will be available for free download to registered customers at saturnbay.ca.

Comments and feedback regarding this book may be submitted through the contact information page on the book publisher's website - saturnbay.ca.

Legend

The legend in Figure 2 is used to represent the charts for the project and product delivery management.

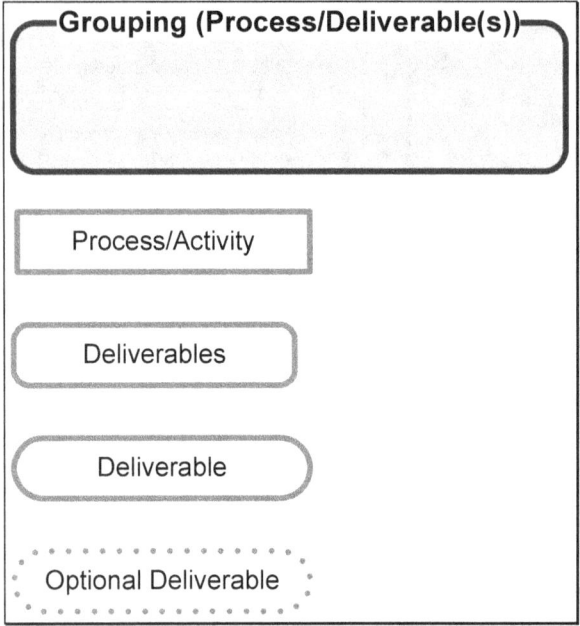

Figure 2 - Legend

Target Audience

This book is for the executives, business managers, project management professionals, training institutions, organizations and those who require concise, definitive and effective practical processes, techniques, tools, templates and good practices to deliver successful projects at all times.

It is for those who are serious about consistently delivering projects successfully. If the processes, techniques, tools and good practices presented are seriously considered and applied, you will reap many benefits.

Specifically, the following groups will find this book a valuable resource to learn, refresh and sharpen their understanding of project management in the context of the overall business strategy, management and operations:

- Business executives and managers.

- Project managers/leaders - new, intermediate and experience levels.

- Project team members - subject matter experts, engineers, architects, business analysts, policy analysts and other professionals who perform activities that contribute to achieving the desired project outcome.

- Students and training institutions - for learning and teaching project management practice.

Caution – What you will get

"Great spirits have always found violent opposition from mediocrities. The latter cannot understand it when a man does not thoughtlessly submit to hereditary prejudices but honestly and courageously uses his intelligence."   *Albert Einstein*

Having a big picture is great. However, if you cannot manage small things, which constitute or make up the big thing, effectively you will be making it challenging to realize your vision and goals. If you cannot manage a project successfully, managing a program and portfolio could be a nightmare, leading to frustration. Effective strategic thinking and actions, and effective project management complements each other.

No single book or any amount of reading can make you a seasoned project manager or business manager. However, good practical books, like this one, can enhance your practice. This will enable you to consistently deliver projects successfully.

You may find things in this book that you really like or disagree with, particularly those things that may seem out of the norm. I acknowledge and respect basic principles, scholars' contributions and diverse opinions. However, I like to think outside the box sometimes and share things that I have tried, some of which may not be familiar to some, but of great value to delivering successful outcomes. You may treat them as the personal opinion or advice of the author, which is subjected to challenge like any other expression of knowledge and experience.

My promise: You will find this book to be one of the most effective and useful practical guide on project management; a perfect addition to your library.

Enjoy!

Blank page

Part 2: Introduction

"Out of intense complexities, intense simplicities emerge."   ***Winston Churchill***

A reasonable understanding of strategy and portfolio management facilitates good understanding and appreciation of the importance of projects and project management. A project manager should understand the need for a project, its purpose, value creation and contribution to strategic agenda of the organization. This part provides a brief overview of strategy and portfolio management, and how they drive the delivery of projects, including the connections between them. Specifically, it includes the following topics:

- Strategy Overview

- Portfolio Management

- Project

- Project Management

Blank page

Chapter 3 - Strategy Overview

"Large views always triumph over small ideas."   ***Winston Churchill***

Business Strategy - Definition and Description

The purpose of this section is to describe the impact of strategy on determining, establishing and committing to the right projects and allocate scarce resources accordingly. Practically, the organization strategy drives the choice of projects. The right projects will deliver the strategic vision and goals of the organization.

Strategy is determined based on the outcome of the analysis of the distinctive and reproducible internal organization capabilities, expressed as strengths and weaknesses, and external environment factors, expressed as opportunities and threats. Strategy planning uses combination of techniques and tools to develop options and make informed decisions on how to take advantage of strengths and opportunities and respond to weaknesses and threats.

The goals of strategy include ensuring effectiveness of service delivery, profitability and, establishing and sustaining competitive advantage. These goals are achieved by developing agendas and action plans that will maintain product/service quality at a lower cost or improve product/service quality at the current or lower cost.

The value of strategy in an enterprise is to maximize profit and prevent or minimize losses, particularly in profit making organizations. Strategy is usually done at the corporate and strategic business units (SBUs) levels. SBU strategies are derived from the corporate strategy. A strategic business unit could be a product line, a service division, a geographical division etc. In the public sector, the corporate strategy is usually derived from the government agenda for its citizens, and the strategic business units could be the ministries, divisions, agencies or program areas. Other levels in the organization derive their plans, programs and projects, from the corporate and SBU strategies.

Strategy Model

Different models are used to develop strategies. A model enables clear thinking and well thought-out approach to managing the various factors, issues and implications of strategic activities and making sense of the complexities involved. A practical and versatile strategy model is a combination of different school of strategic thoughts, which include planning, learning, design, positioning, and social-cultural factors. The model in Figure 3 depicts this practical concept.

The strategists, usually business owners and executives, define the vision and agendas that drive the organization business activities. The vision drives the strategic choices of the organization. Strategy is not just about setting a vision, planning and forecasting, to maintain control. A sustainable strategy is determined by the organization's ability to respond to predictable and unpredictable changes in the internal and external factors.

Analysis and diagnosis involve the examination of technological, organizational and environmental factors, which impact the organization performance and desired outcome. Internal factors include organization competences, policies and resources (i.e. human capital, financial, assets etc.). External factors include political, legal, economical, physical, competitive and related issues. Comprehensive analysis of the internal and external factors determines the organization SWOT (strengths, weaknesses, opportunities and threats). The SWOT report provides the required information for determining the preferred strategy or combination of strategies for the organization.

The chosen strategy drives the organization governance, structure and resource allocations, required to implement the strategy. The implementation needs to be evaluated and controlled to ensure that the organization is on track to meet its strategic goals.

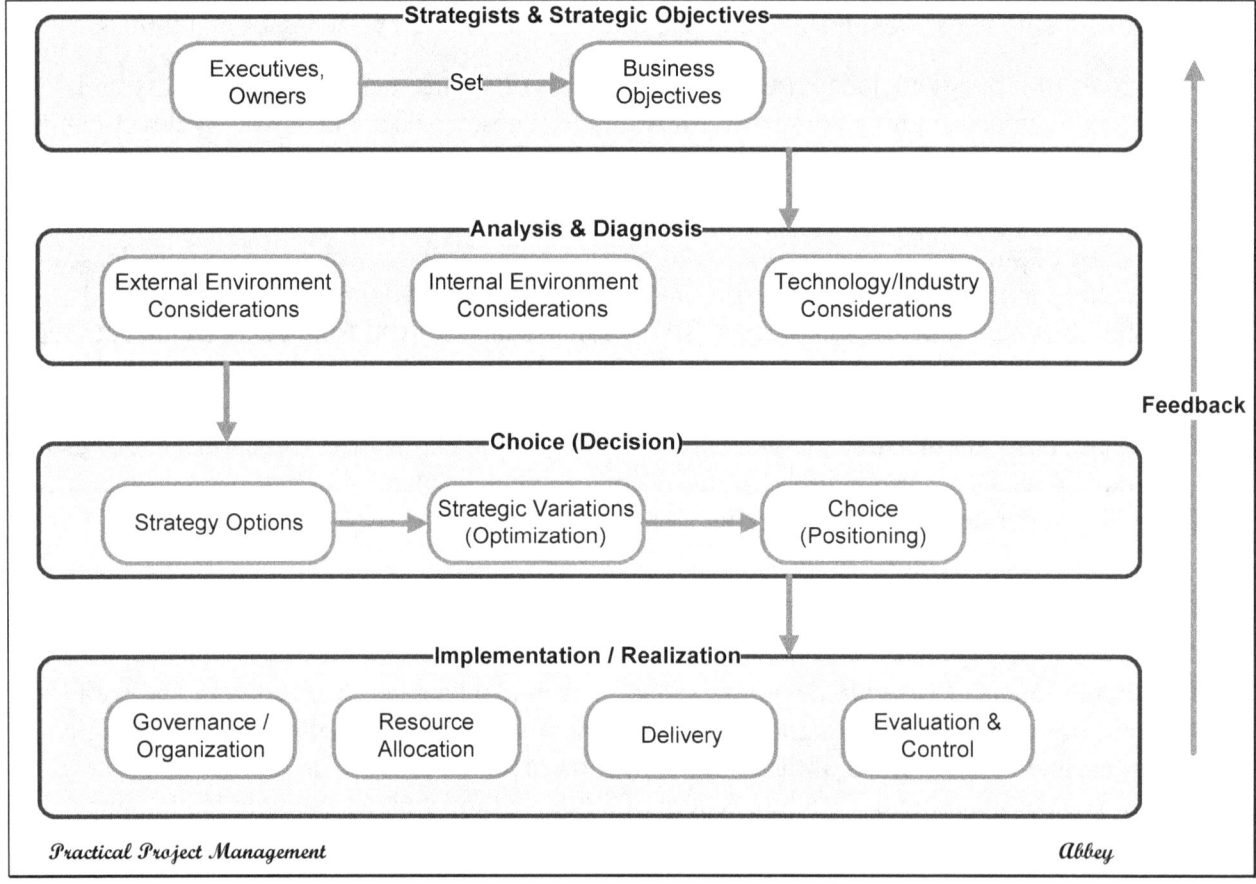

Figure 3 - A Strategy Model

A learning organization promotes lessons learnt through effective engagement of stakeholders and an established feedback process to ensure free flow of information. An effective feedback process enables the development of a flexible strategy that responds to the constantly changing internal and external factors. An effective strategy requires involvement of all stakeholders to a varying degree and at different stages. A clear and reliable feedback from the stakeholders will keep the strategy alive, make it effective and responsive to change. The effectiveness of obtaining timely feedback, from the portfolio, project and operations domains, will enable the organization to respond quickly to new challenges by adjusting the strategy appropriately.

Strategy is like an elephant. You may see or focus on a part of the big picture and easily loose sight of the other parts. The key challenge is to see better and clearer, through practice, rather than relying solely on narrowed vision, experience, techniques and tools. There is no one fit-all situation strategy. Strategy is a flexible but unique endeavour to suitably position the organization to respond to the current and emerging internal and external challenges.

You may reference other organizations' strategies, but trying to copy them could be a recipe for disaster or confusion. A strategy that makes organization 'A' successful may not work for organization 'B'. In practical sense, there is no 'best strategy'; instead, the focus should be on the preferred and appropriate strategy for a specific organization, situation and time.

No matter how smart or solid an organization strategy is, its effectiveness is only evident when the rubber meets the road. A practical strategy is flexible with room for timely feedback from reality and ability to respond quickly with rational changes in the strategy. Strategy drives the portfolio, projects and operational activities that should be established and managed to meet the strategic goals of an organization.

Strategy, Portfolio, Projects and Operations

Figure 4 shows the inter-relationship between strategy, portfolios, projects and operations. The linkage between projects, portfolios and strategy provides a good understanding and importance of projects initiation. As shown in Figure 4, the relationships between strategy, portfolios, projects and operations are multi-dimensional and multi-directional, which enables free flow of information.

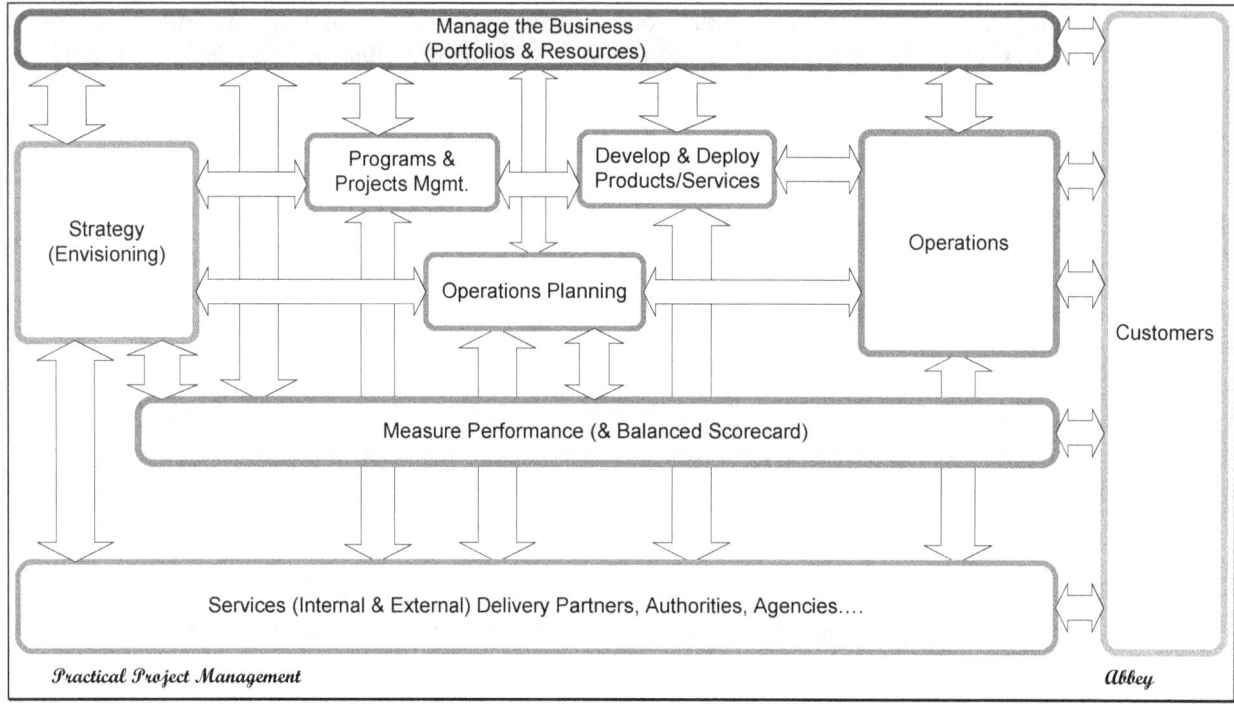

Figure 4 - Strategy-Portfolio-Project-Operations linkage

Chapter 4 - Portfolio Management

Different types of portfolio exist in the business world - financial, system, service and project portfolios are common examples. This book focuses on project portfolio. Project portfolio management is about identifying, assessing, selecting and committing to implement the right projects. The right projects are projects which are in alignment with the organization's strategic goals. Projects are created to facilitate the development of new or enhanced products and services. Project management is about executing the right projects *right*. Implementation of the right projects fulfilled the strategic goals. Portfolio management provides the linkage between the business strategy and project management.

Figure 5 shows the relationship between portfolio, program and projects. A program may contain other programs or sub-programs, projects and other activities (for example, procurement services for supporting the program). The arrows show the directions of the information flow and interactions. Program, in project context, composed of multiple projects to be delivered to achieve common program or strategic goals, which could not be achieved otherwise.

Fulfilling strategic goals require a well planned and managed project portfolio or set of portfolios. Programs, projects and other operational activities are components of a portfolio. Portfolio management facilitates establishing priority across initiatives and determines how best to allocate resources to the initiatives in order to fulfill the organization's strategic goals.

A major activity of portfolio management is the opportunity assessment. Opportunity assessment is the evaluation of every project, group of projects or programs in alignment with the strategic agenda of the organization. Opportunity assessment also considers how the project of interest may impact or relate to other projects, a larger project or program. This assessment uses some key parameters like NPV (Net Present Value), ROI (Return on Investment) and Payback. Also, it considers other factors like impact on jobs, overall economy and social-cultural implications. Definitions of these parameters are provided in the glossary section. Sometimes a project or group of projects may be evaluated in the context of a fundamental business change (i.e. business re-engineering).

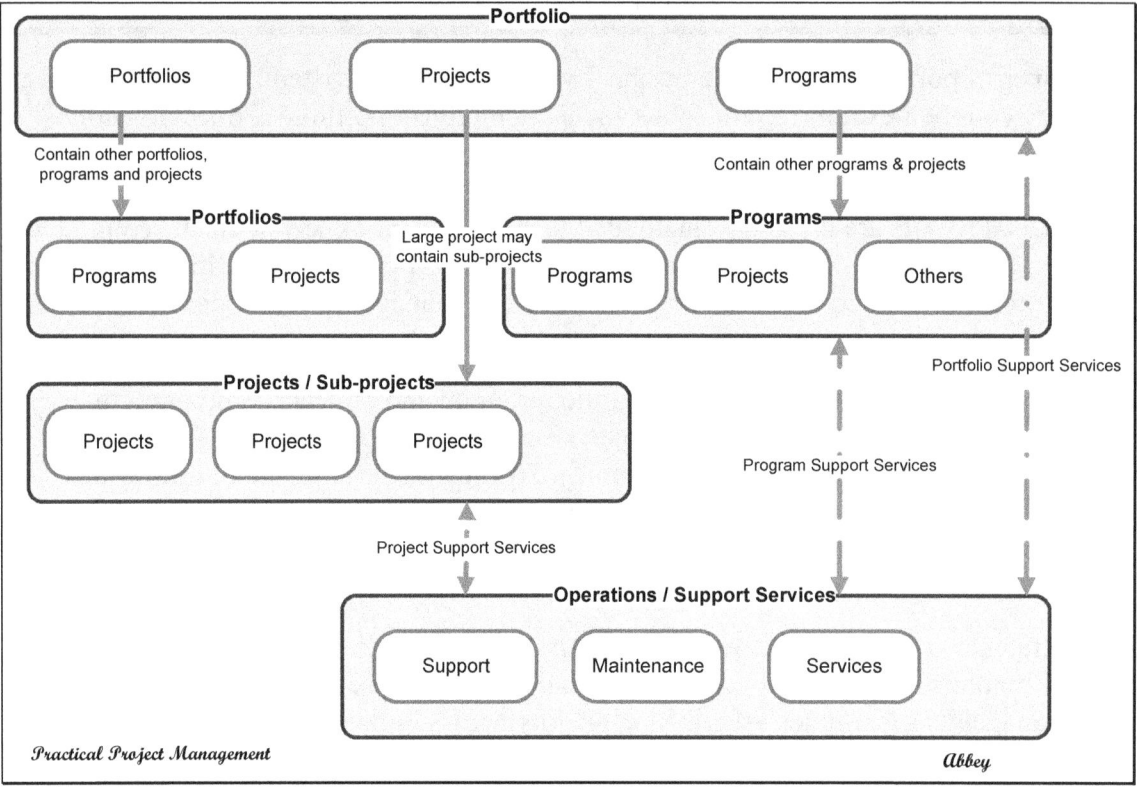

Figure 5 - Project Portfolio, Program and Project Overview

Governance

Governance is the harmonization of processes, roles and responsibilities, and resources to facilitate the successful delivery of projects and other organization activities, including service delivery and customer support. Organizations establish governance at different levels of responsibilities to facilitate service excellence and free information exchange.

Figure 6 shows a governance overview at the corporate, strategic business unit, portfolio, project and operational levels, and the relationship between them. A well thought-out governance facilitates successful delivery of projects. Effective, performing and value driven organizations ensure that governance at different levels have clearly defined interfaces with unambiguous roles and responsibilities. The goal is to maximize scarce resources and reduce product delivery turn-around time or time to the market.

Leadership discipline across the organization facilitates value creation and organization effectiveness. A project manager should understand the established organization governance in order to manage project effectively. Also, to enable the successful delivery of projects, ensure the establishment of steering groups with authority to make timely decisions. A typical project governance is shown in Figure 35 (see page 127).

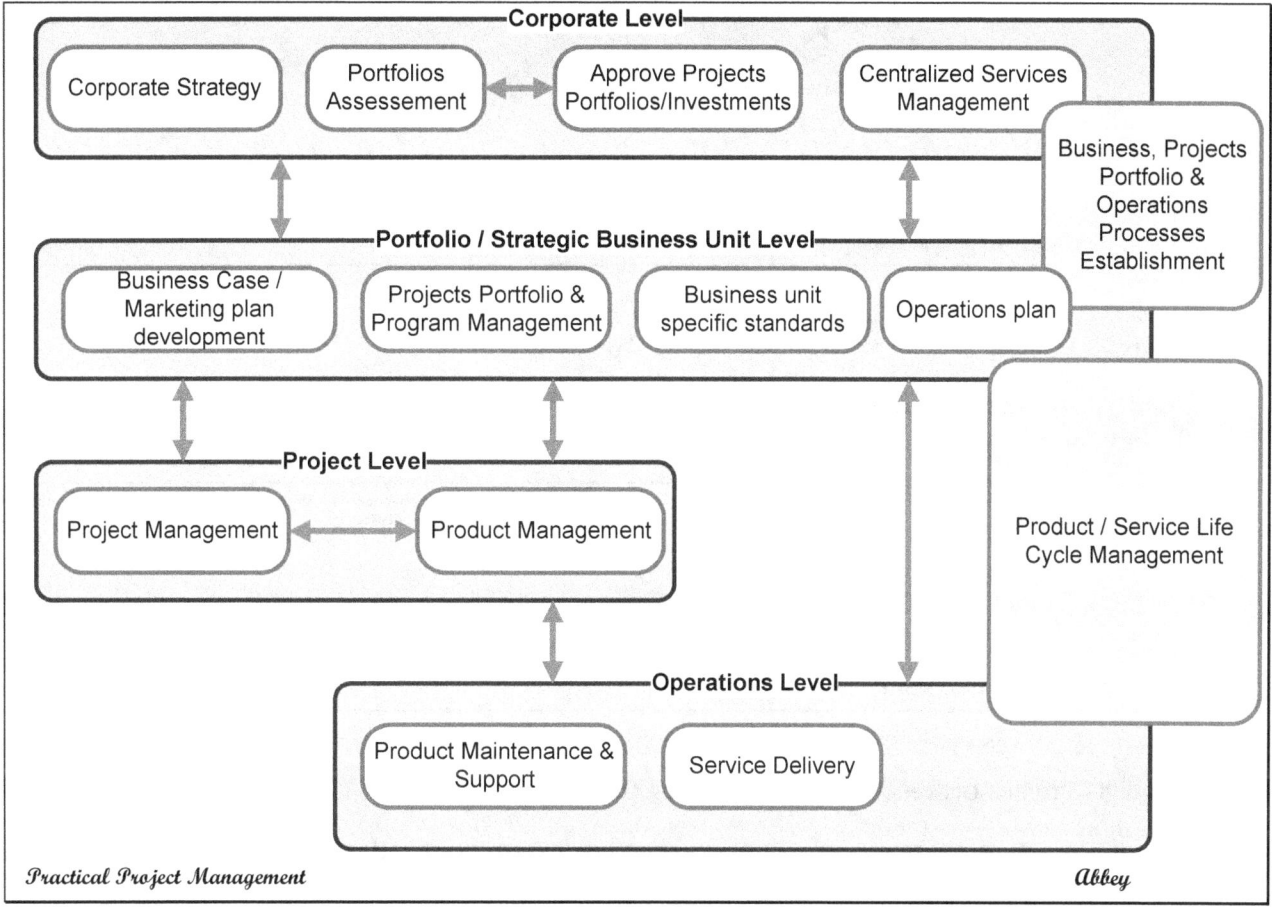

Figure 6 - Governance Overview

Gating - Overview and Importance

Gating provides a process for tracking the performance, value and current relevance of a project or group of projects vis-à-vis the current strategic reality, which is influenced by the organizational and environmental factors. It is critical to the realization of the business strategic goals. Dynamic organizations will assess the viability of projects, in terms of cost and benefits, on a regular basis. Figure 7 shows a typical gating process for the project portfolio management.

Each organization may have its own customized version of the gating process. The important thing to know is that gating provides a practical approach to consistently evaluate and validate the credibility, relevance and viability of projects during the product development stages.

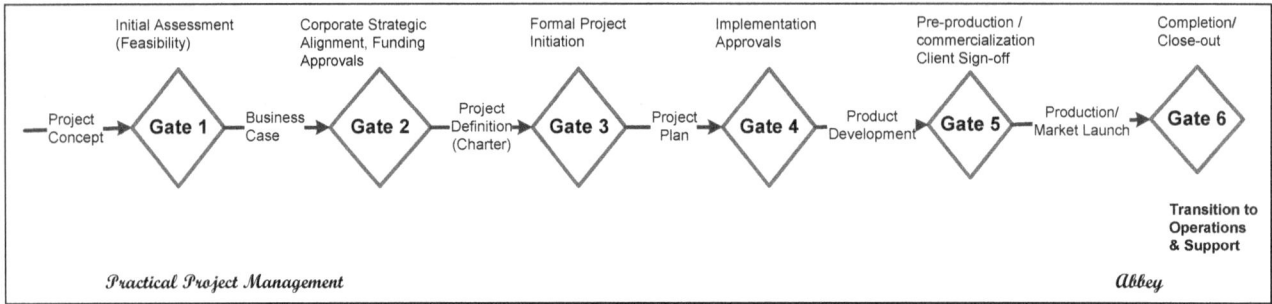

Figure 7 - Project Portfolio Management Gating Overview

Figure 8 shows the gating process specific to the product delivery management, particularly for new products.

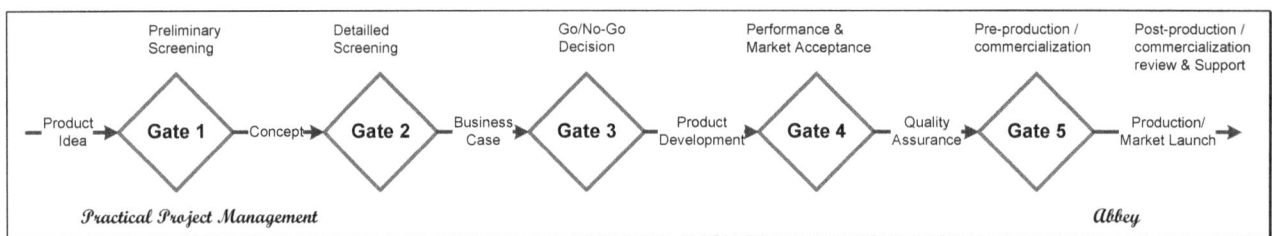

Figure 8 - Product Delivery Management Gating Overview

The product delivery management gating can be described as follows:

Gate 1 - the initial screening determines the ideas strategic fit.

Gate 2 - the preliminary assessments of the ideas to determine technical and market feasibility.

Gate 3 - the more detailed version of gate 2. The main activity following gate 3 is the design and development of the product and a marketing plan.

Gate 4 - deals with the assessment of the product performance, the likely market acceptance of the product, and whether the degree of the market acceptance is sufficient to justify further development.

Gate 5 - the product is subjected to a test market (laboratory or field test, cash permitting) or pilot. The outcome of the testing or pilot determines the 'go/no-go' commercialization decision.

Most initiatives or ideas are stopped at the initial stage, a less costly undertaking than stopping the initiatives at a later stage. Gating provides a practical way to prevent committing much resource to projects that may never make it to the commercialization or production stage. Gating can be used to optimize scarce resources, maximize profit or minimize losses.

Business case and marketing plan will be briefly discussed next. Other key deliverables for the gating process will be discussed in the project management and product delivery management sections. Business case or marketing plan provides key information for developing other deliverables, mainly project charter and integrated project plan.

Chapter 5 – Portfolio Opportunity Assessment

Business Case

In order to approve a project for implementation, a business case or opportunity assessment document is required to justify the need for the project. Some organizations will extend this to marketing plan, which include opportunity assessment and commercialization plan. Business case demonstrates the need and strategic importance or relevance of the project. That is, it demonstrates the alignment of the proposed project to the organization strategy. Usually every project is assessed within a portfolio and compared to other projects in terms of the value creation, strategic alignment and opportunity cost. Opportunity cost is the cost of the best alternative forgone.

A business case includes the following:

- Assessment of the current situation, including issues, internal and external environmental factors (organization capability, political, economy, social, legal etc.).

- Vision, goals, desired outcome and deliverables.

- Analysis of options - includes considerations of resource requirements, deliverables, estimates of cost and benefits, return on investment, net present value and investment payback (i.e. time to recover implementation cost).

- Recommendations - are based on the outcome of the options analysis and other considerations like social, political and physical environment factors.

- Implementation strategy - includes the governance, timeline, transition and post-implementation review plans.

Once the business case is approved and funding provided, a term of reference or a project charter is created to define the project agenda in a clearer detail. Prior to the wide adoption of project management methodologies, some organizations create a term of reference (TOR) to indicate business case acceptance and approval to proceed with the initiative implementation. This type of TOR is usually smaller in size or content than a typical project charter.

For small projects, a TOR may suffice for the project charter. To initiate a project, a term of reference (TOR) or charter is required. The charter defines the mandate and scope statements, guides and drives the project implementation, and enables the project manager to develop a clear road map to fulfill the goals and needs of the project.

Essentially, a TOR includes the following:

- Vision, objectives, scope and deliverables (what)

- Key stakeholders, their interests, roles and responsibilities (who)

- Resources required - money, human and materials; and approach (how)

- Expected delivery date, timeline (when)

A project charter include the above and more (risk management, change management, governance etc.). Project charter will be discussed in the subsequent section.

Marketing Plan

A marketing plan is a vital document that guides the successful and profitable delivery of a new or enhanced product. It is required to demonstrate the viability and commercialization potential of the product. The viability or opportunity assessment component of a marketing plan is equivalent to the business case. Business case may suffice to justify an initiative that requires funding within the organization. However, marketing plan is essential to secure an initiative funding from external sources (for example, financial institutions). Sometimes, marketing plan is referred to as a business plan, particularly for a single product or product line organization. A marketing plan is more elaborate than a business case, and could suffice for a business case. A strategic business unit within an organization develops marketing plan to demonstrate the alignment of its products and services with the corporate strategy and compete for scarce resources.

A marketing plan includes the opportunity assessment and commercialization plan. Opportunity assessment is the analysis of the organization capability, customers, competitive and environmental factors. Commercialization plan includes the combination of product, pricing, promotion and distribution strategies. A critical success factor for an effective marketing plan is creating a superior product for an attractive market, where there is little or no competition, with strong marketing capabilities.

A marketing plan includes the following:

- Corporate strategy statement - vision, objectives and strategic direction.

- Opportunity assessment - also called the 4Cs (Customer or target market, environment Considerations, organization Capabilities and Competition). It also addresses current situations and keys issues. The main output of the opportunity assessment is the SWOT (strengths, weaknesses, opportunities and threats) report.

- Marketing strategies - also called the 4Ps (Product, Pricing, Promotion and Place or distribution strategies). These are the realistic and thought-out strategies that take advantage of strengths and opportunities, and respond to weaknesses and threats.

- Action plan - includes resource allocation and implementation timeline.

- Financial statements - includes capital outlay, income (profit & loss), balance sheet and cash flow projections.

- Control & contingencies - includes organization governance and structure, risk management and contingency plan, legal issues, communication plan, performance tracking and auditing of the ongoing health check for the various components of the marketing plan.

A sample marketing plan outline used to build the marketing strategy for this book is shown in Figure 9. It serves well as a template to brainstorm and build a comprehensive marketing plan. A marketing plan, if approved, provides the initiation and mandate for the project delivery, including the development of associated artefacts, mainly the project charter and integrated project plan.

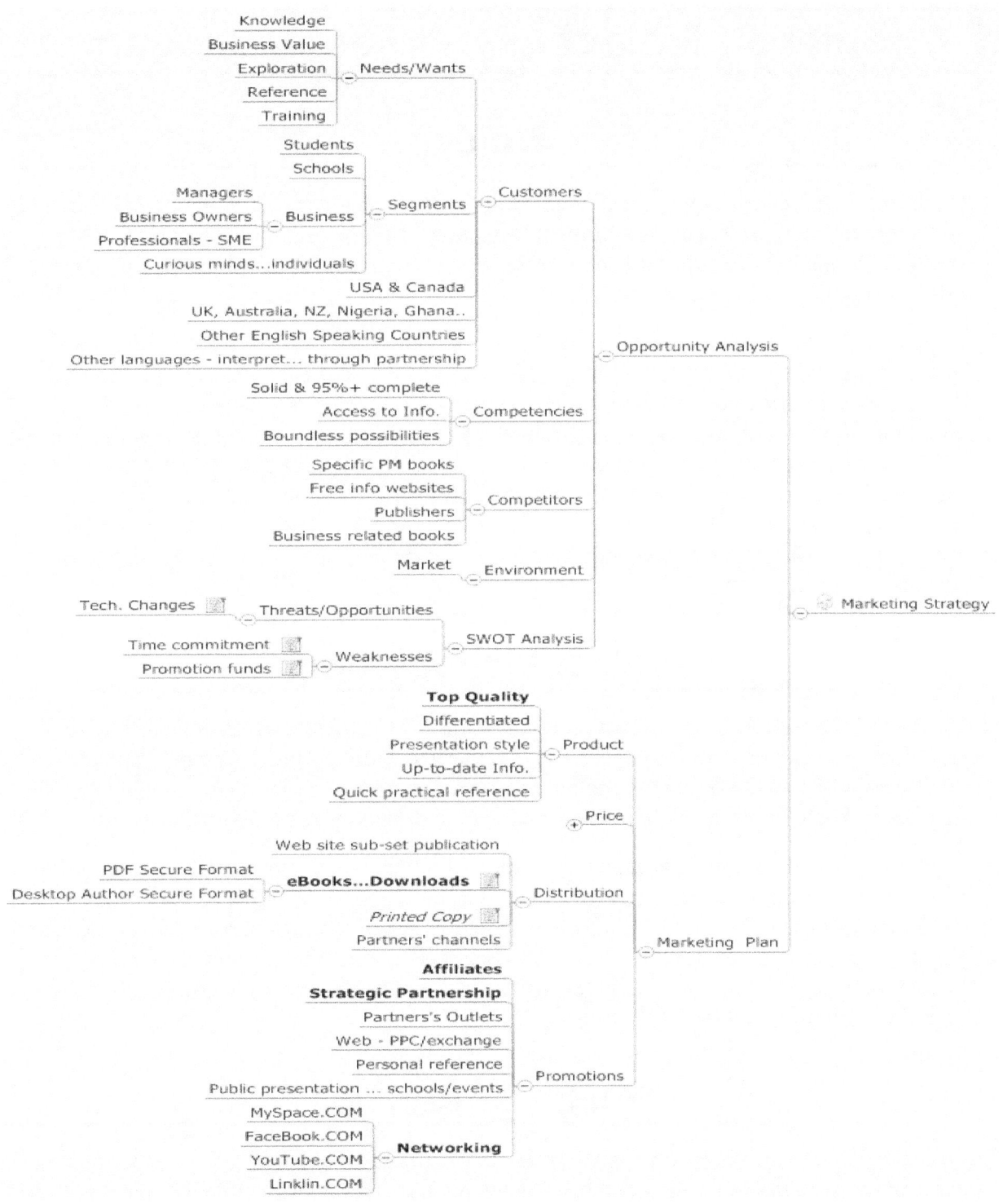

Figure 9 - Marketing Plan Outline – An Example

Chapter 6 - Project and Project Management

Project

A project is defined as a specific piece of work or a unique endeavour with defined start and end dates, requiring resource commitment to accomplish the desired result or outcome. The goal of a project is to deliver product(s) or service(s) at a pre-defined quality within approved time and budget.

Depending on the organization or project owner, any event, activity or major undertaking, that meet the above project definition, could be regarded as a project. Some organizations classify most activities or undertakings as project items in order to ensure consistent coordination, tracking, monitoring and control of cost, time and quality. For example, an on-going activity may be setup as a yearly project with established time & budget. Other organizations consider only major undertakings of certain durations (for example, 30 days or more) as projects, and other activities as regular operational activities. The key consideration is to ensure consistent, clear and understandable criteria for defining and establishing an undertaking as a project item.

Project Management

Project management is a discipline that involves planning, organizing and controlling of resources (human, materials, equipment and money) to fulfil the project goals. It is the engagement of suitable resources and application of processes, techniques and tools to plan, manage and deliver project deliverables, which deliver the desired outcome.

A project is faced with key traditional constraints - scope (what), time (when) and cost (how much) to accomplish a corresponding product quality. These constraints need to be appraised at the initial stage and at every point where change is required to the agreed and approved project scope or when an unplanned situation occurs (for example, an unexpected risk). Delivering a project on time, on budget and to meet the desired quality are the key measures of project delivery success.

Project Categories

Projects can be placed in thee categories: transformational, maintenance and support. These categories are guides only for understanding a typical project, its strategic placement and importance within an organization.

Transformational projects: These are projects initiated to create new or modified products or services. The goal is to implement change and deliver value to the organization and clients. Examples include new road construction, a real estate project, a new gas plant, a new product and a new service centre.

Maintenance projects: These are projects initiated to sustain existing products or services that are still within their life cycle, and are considered relevant to the continued existence of the organization or its services to the clients. Examples include existing road maintenance, home renovations, system maintenance and refinery turn-around maintenance.

Support projects: A project is considered a support project, when its needs and funding solely depend on another project. A support project is approved based on the value it creates for and its strategic importance to the delivery of the main project. Examples include the telecommunication system for a new payment solution and a new road leading to a new production facility.

Chapter 7 - Why Projects Succeed or Fail

Whether a project succeeds or fails, the organization will reap the rewards of positive outcome or have to deal with the consequences of failure. A project may be cancelled in order to minimize losses, particularly if the project is no longer relevant or not able to deliver the expected value. A project cancelled for this reason may not be considered a failure. A value or profit driven organization understands that the success of a project requires the collaborative effort and commitments of the stakeholders.

The beginning of a project is usually about laying the foundation for the project success. Most projects that succeed or fail occur at the beginning, and failure can be prevented if warning signals are not ignored or swept under the carpet. However, there are instances where projects fail during the implementation phase due to various reasons such as poor handling and lack of stakeholders', particularly the executives', support. The following list is not exhaustive but provides some insight into why projects succeed or fail.

Why Projects Succeed?

Projects success could be attributed to various factors, including the following:

- ***Projects aligned with the strategic organization goals*** and with full executive commitment and support.

- ***Committed, skilled, adaptable and resourceful professional project teams and members*** who take responsibilities for assigned work packages, activities and tasks, and prepared to work as a team.

- ***Well initiated projects*** that have clearly defined and formally approved terms of reference.

- ***Well managed and executed projects*** based on realistic planning.

- ***Adopt respectful debates to resolve problems***, issues and conflicts.

- Establishment of a ***service oriented project team*** and a supportive governance.

- ***Relevant, regular and timely communication*** with the stakeholders on progress status, performance, issues and outcomes.

- ***Good and complementary practices*** across the organization. These practices will be discussed further in the future sections.

Why Projects Fail?

Project failure could be attributed to the following - people, product design, decision making, partnership, supplier and project management discipline problems.

- *Excessive politics:* This may involve taking steps that are not aligned with the organization strategic goals. For example, implementing a project that makes the team performance looks better but put the organization at a disadvantage. Some executives promote personal interests rather than initiatives that promote the organizational growth and competitiveness. This could occur in organizations where they are not held accountable by stakeholders and shareholders. It could sometimes be due to principal-agent or conflict of interest problem. These situations may not occur in a service oriented organization, where team performance is tied to the organization success.

- *Lack of executive commitment and/or sponsorship*; lack of clear vision, enthusiasm, will and focus, as well as conflicting and unrealistic priorities. Do not commit scarce resources to a project if you are not sure of its relevance to the organization strategic goals.

- *Ineffective governance and lack of shared responsibility and accountability*. This could be caused by lousy project management, absence of leadership discipline or lack of executive commitment to providing needed support in resolving escalated issues in a timely fashion.

- *Battle of egos and unhealthy competition*: Particularly with problem solving, issues and conflict resolutions. Battle of ego is sometimes caused by the desire of team members to outshine one another. Some project team members or stakeholders do not realize how transient their role is either on a project or even in an operational environment. When project team members realize that they are just fulfilling a transient role which could change with future assignments, battle of ego problem may diminish.

- *Undervalued work force*: Unfair treatment of the organization's workforce or project resource could be devastating for the whole organization. This is not a problem in a truly service oriented organization, where the main focus of everyone in the organization and their performance is solely based on results.

- *Indecisive and unprofessional project managers*: Sometimes, some project managers fail to show courage, decisiveness and tenacity to get things done even in the face of adversity. Successful project managers show good judgment and are decisive, tenacious and result driven.

- *Unrealistic expectations and assigning insufficient and/or incapable resources to projects*. Resource assignment impacts the amount of effort, cost and quality of outcome. Inadequate and incapable resources could result in project delivery failure or unnecessary delay.

- ***Blame culture and lack of shared ownership:*** In organizations where blame culture is a common practice, project team members, particularly the junior members, are afraid to be creative and take risks that could enhance the project team performance and deliver positive outcome.

Chapter 8 – Facts and Myths about Project Management

Some facts and myths about project management are described below:

- ***Project manager is accountable for the successful delivery of the project.*** This is true. However, the whole team and organization will reap the benefits of the project success and bear the burden of project failure. Therefore, the key stakeholders of the project will be better off by taking shared ownership and shared responsibilities for the project success. As a project manager, take charge and engage others as partners, and promote shared ownership and responsibilities in order to ensure successful delivery of the project.

- ***A project delivered on time and budget is a sign of successful project delivery and maturity***. Sometimes the heroic effort of one or few of the project team members can ensure timely project completion. However, this is not a sustainable practice. Assembling the right, committed and disciplined resources for the project is the key to the success of the project.

- ***A good project manager tries to please the client by avoiding saying 'NO'.*** This is an unrealistic and self defeating attitude. A mature and result oriented project manager learns how to say no with style, for instance you could make a statement like: if the A, B and C conditions are met, we may be able to do this and that, turning the situation into a negotiation, as there are different options to solving a problem or resolving an issue. You can turn an emphatic no into possibilities with conditions. Remember, negotiation is a key decision making tool in project management. You cannot and should not (always) be dictated to or instructed. For example, a change to the project scope needs to go through the change management process in order to understand the impact of the change and get it approved by authorized stakeholders.

- ***Be optimistic and you will be fine.*** I like being optimistic, albeit cautiously, and I do not encourage pessimism. However, it is advisable to be realistic about project management and respect differed opinions as part of the overall effort to ensure successful delivery of projects. It is important to be realistic about project scope, associated cost and time, applicable technology and value creation.

- ***Ensure quick delivery, compress time and be aggressive***. Be careful, ensure that the key players understand what is required of them and commit to a realistic time to deliver. Of course, as an entry strategy, you may put forward a tight schedule to prevent slackness from others. Unrealistic schedule leads to constant shifting of target dates. The key here is openness and clarity of work description, delivery expectations and realistic estimation, based on experience and good judgment.

- ***Defend your position at all cost***. This is not professional, particularly when you are in a hole stop digging. Debate does not imply blindly misrepresenting information. Whoever recognizes his/her limits, will seek and receive help. He who is not ready and willing to learn cannot be counseled.

- ***Lessons learnt sessions should be conducted at the end of the project***. You may forget important lessons if you follow this rule. It is advisable to make lessons learnt part of your regular project management activities. You may conduct a short informal lessons learnt session after the completion of a work package or a major activity.

- ***Enforce methodology at all times***. Realistically, in some organizations, a project manager is chosen before a project is formally initiated, funding approved and project charter completed. This may not be a bad practice as long as the project manager is not required or mandated to commit to deliver project outcome, prior to the formal initiation point. Choosing a project manager earlier could afford him/her some advantages - influence preliminary planning activities (funding, business case and project charter development), acquire early understanding and take control of the project.

- ***Clients require a competent and strong project manager***. The truth is, sometimes, when a strong, disciplined and professional project manager joins the team, he/she meets strong resistance. Project managers who are not strong and competent may find themselves standing for nothing or delivering mediocre result, at best. All organizations, teams and individuals are not the same. Be yourself, be strong, be focused and aim for gold in your project management discipline. Your effort will surely be appreciated and rewarded by those who value your candor and substance.

- ***Your understanding of what you say or communicate might be different from the understanding of your audience***. It is practically impossible for anyone to clarify every spoken word, but ensure you clarify your stakeholders' understanding of what is expected of you and of them.

- ***Claiming to know everything is the beginning of (and lead to more) ignorance. There is no harm in saying I don't know***. This could make you look like a fool once, but claiming to know when you don't could make you a fool forever. Those claiming to know it all cannot be counseled. Ask questions, and you shall receive answers from willing and able minds.

- ***The true cost of a project is established after the close of the project***. This is true. However, wide discrepancies in cost, time and quality will not be entertained by the client and could make you lose respect, except in an evidently unusual or rare situation that is usually beyond project control.

- ***Lowest bidder is preferred.*** 'Caveat emptor' (buyer beware); you will get what you paid for.

Part 3: Approach

This part describes the service oriented delivery approach to managing project, and the importance of emphasizing the management of projects and products delivery as services. The following topics are discussed:

- Why Service Oriented Approach?
- Service Life Cycle
- Project and Product Delivery Management
- Good Practices
- Complementary Practices

Blank page

Chapter 9 - Why Service Oriented Approach?

"Out of intense complexities, intense simplicities emerge."   *Winston Churchill*

A service oriented approach is about the delivery of a piece of work, product or service, through the collaborative effort of the organization's teams, whose performances and rewards are tied to the outcomes of the project. In situations where the team effort is more rewarded than personal effort, team members support and challenge each other. This leads to healthy competition, promotes creativity, prevents groupthink (that is, complacency and conformity among the team members). A service oriented team resolves issues faster and is a catalyst for service excellence.

Having a service oriented mind set enables the organization and the project team to understand the strategic importance of an undertaking and focus on delivering an outcome that relies on the collaborative effort, not heroic or individual effort.

A service oriented approach can also be described in terms of the concept of boundary-less information flow. Boundary-less information flow enables independent systems, teams and organizations to work together seamlessly, with clear exchange or free flow of information in every direction.

Service oriented organizations organize their resources around the product or service they produce, sell and support. These organizations make conscious effort to establish objective measures that are used to measure the success of the desired outcome throughout the value chain - that is, every point where contributions are made to deliver the end product. A service oriented approach ensures the establishment of a clear pathway from conception to realization, sustenance and retirement. Service oriented organizations have gained distinctive capabilities and competitive advantages in their industries and in the marketplace.

Service oriented organizations base rewards on results and in proportion to the contributions of the teams, without ignoring the individual contribution. Rewards solely based on individual performance could cause unhealthy competition, promotes empire building, protectionism or self preservation and conflicting performance measures.

A traditional or non-service oriented organization is a highly stressed environment and less innovative. It is characterized by blame culture, high conflicts, groupthink, unhealthy competition, uncontrolled escalations, low productivity, complacency and mediocrity. In a traditional organization, getting things done depends heavily on who knows who.

Service oriented organizations are usually the best performing organizations. They focus on developing people and teams that create superior solutions and services, and build wealth. Their workforces are happier, more productive and less stressed; they know and recognize their value to the organization and count on each other to deliver results.

Chapter 10 - Service Life Cycle

Most organizations have established processes for project management, product delivery management and service management. However, a complete and harmonized framework that combines these processes rarely exists. A key challenge is taking ownership of the combined processes, due to the frictions that exist at the interfaces between them. Service life cycle helps to resolve this challenge by establishing a harmonized framework, including the supporting governance, to ensure the consistent end-to-end delivery and sustenance of products or services.

Understanding and embracing service life cycle facilitates effective product or service design, development, delivery, support, and retirement. Service life cycle provides a preferred way to measure and understand total cost of ownership of delivering a product or service. Figure 10 shows a service life cycle framework, which can be customized or used as a reference to develop an organization service life cycle framework.

The service life cycle framework in Figure 10 includes the supporting governance, stages and performance assessment steps to achieve service excellence. An organization service life cycle framework, with the supporting governance, provides clarity on teams interactions, roles and responsibility. A practical service life cycle framework facilitates stakeholders' collaboration to produce superior results.

Supporting governance includes corporate/service strategy, service portfolio management, service delivery management and service operations management. Service strategy defines the organization's service delivery vision, goals and strategic choices. Service portfolio management includes project and product portfolios management. Service delivery management includes product/service design, development and delivery. Service operations management includes product/service operations, post-delivery support and retirement. Product/service renewal requires the collaboration of service portfolio management, service delivery management and service operations management.

In a service oriented organization, a practical service life cycle framework facilitates single point of accountability and/or responsibility. Team performance reward is paramount, without diminishing or eliminating individual performance reward. When deliverables are assigned, the assignee is responsible for completing it as agreed and gets support from others as needed. This diminishes the emphasis on job description and enables team members to focus their efforts on delivering results. Team members are willing to make things work. A service oriented approach has proven to deliver greater successes than other alternatives.

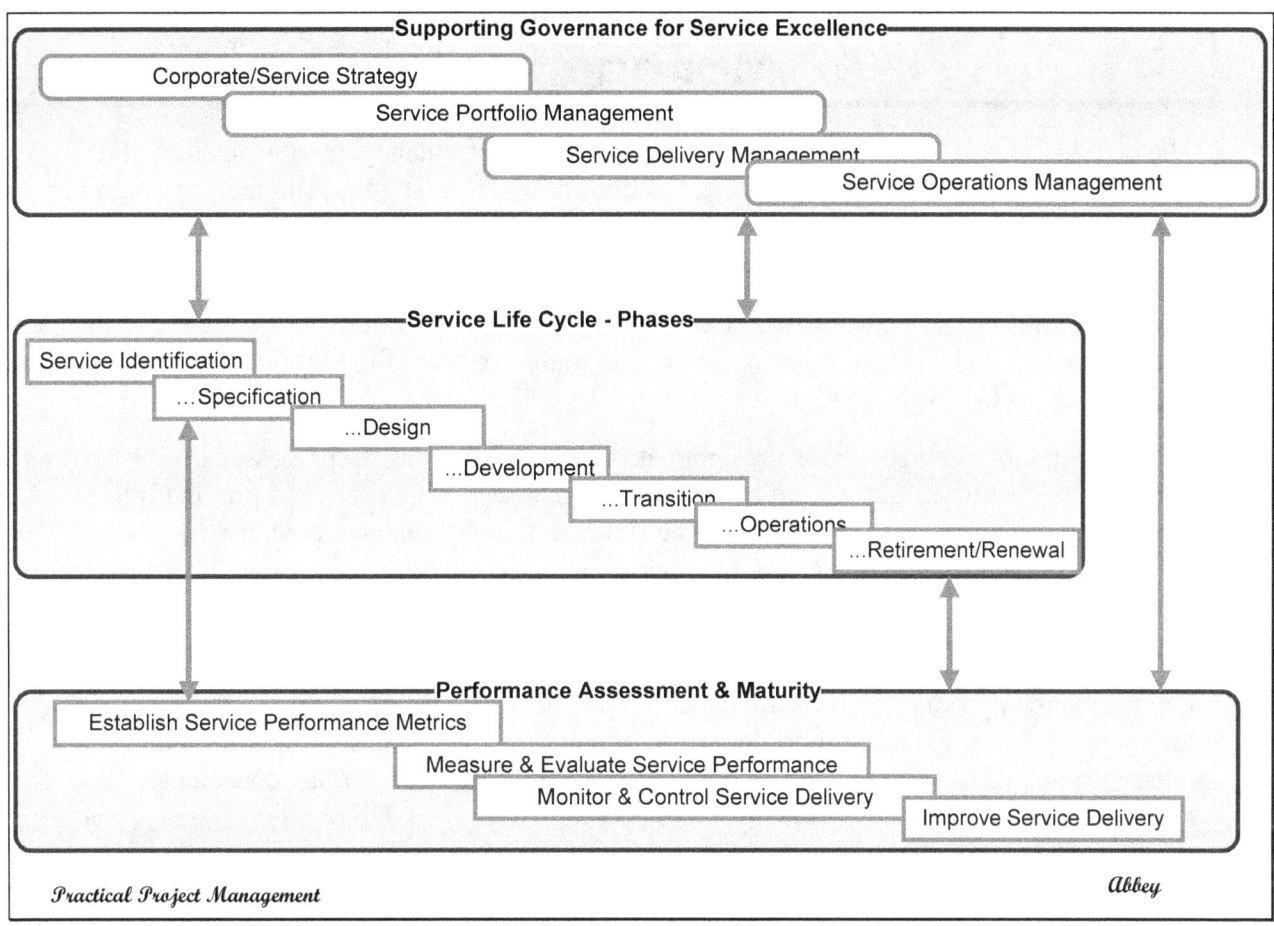

Figure 10 - Service Life Cycle

Chapter 11 - Project and Product Delivery Management

The emphasis on project management and product delivery management is to show the importance of the subject matter expertise required in each discipline and their overlapping relationships that are required to deliver the desired project outcome.

Project management is the discipline of planning, controlling, monitoring, executing and closing a project. It provides management oversight for product delivery. A project manager does not have to be, and not usually, the subject matter expert of the product the project has been mandated to develop and deliver.

Product delivery management is the application of specific industry processes or frameworks to obtain and analyze product requirements, design, develop and deliver a product into a production or commercialization state. The product delivery management processes are layered with the project management processes, and together they provide a unified delivery methodology.

Product delivery management delivers the outcome of the project through effective project management. A product delivery manager, responsible for the product delivery, is usually a lead subject matter expert or a product development lead who has solid end-to-end understanding of the product design and development processes. He/she coordinates the design and development resource efforts to accomplish project delivery goals. For projects with simplified requirements and lower risks, the same person may play both the role of the project manager and the product delivery manager.

Figure 11 shows the relationship between project management and product delivery management. The goal of project management is to ensure timely and cost effective delivery of a product or set of products. The goal of product delivery management is to deliver the right product in order to fulfill the overall goal of the project. Project management is industry independent; product delivery management is industry specific. Examples of industries include information technology, sales, service, construction, manufacturing - chemicals, pharmaceutical etc.

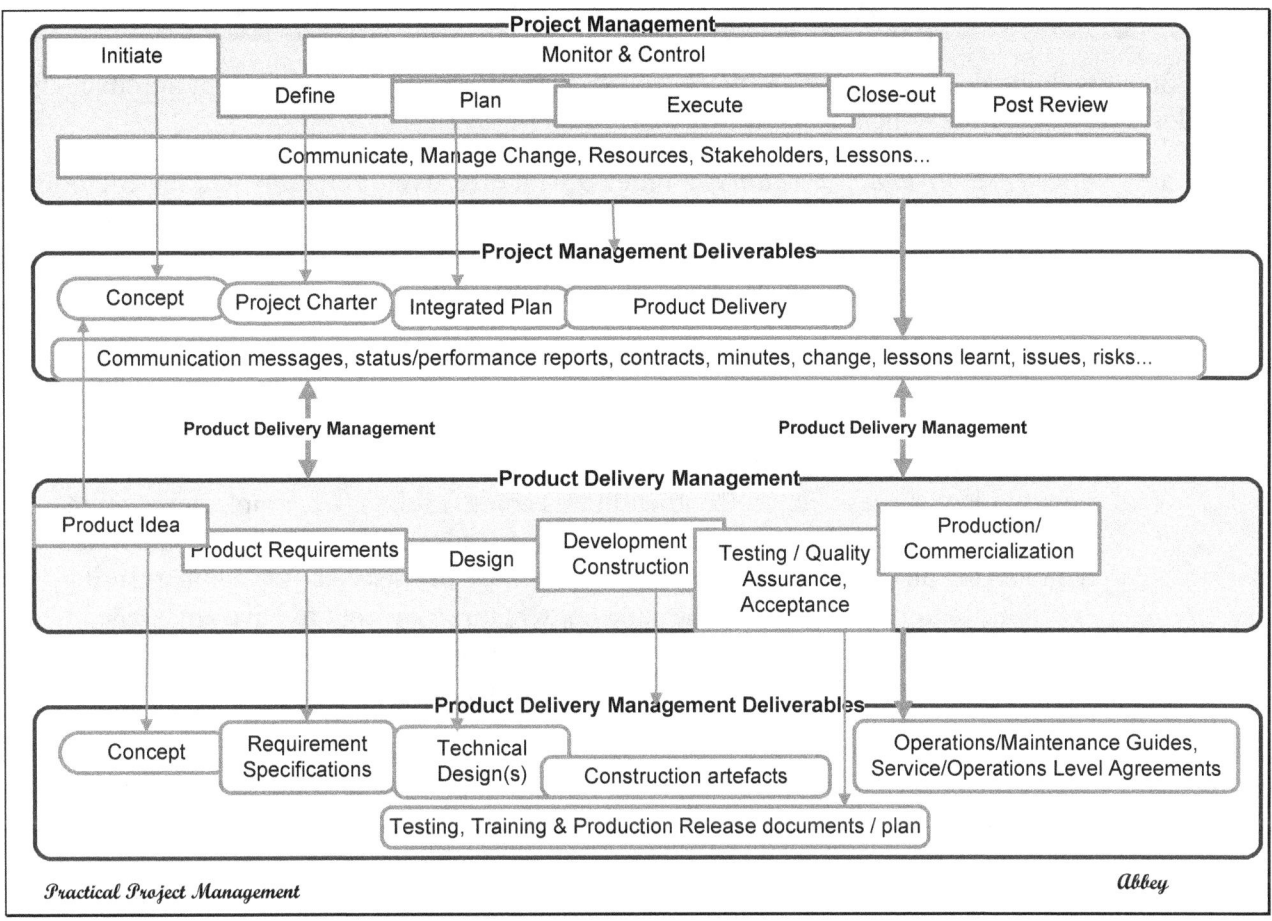

Figure 11 - Project & Product Delivery Management Relationship – An Overview

Chapter 12 - Good Practices

Some good practices that facilitate successful service life cycle management and produce the desired project results include the following:

- *A well established governance* combined with effective, preferably automated, tools to record, track, monitor and ensure accountabilities and responsibilities across the value chain are critical to the success of the service life cycle management, which include project management and product delivery management. The governance should not be based on endless committees, but rather on teams and individuals with well defined roles and responsibilities limited to corporate, strategic business units, project portfolio and project management levels.

- *Having signed contracts among the key players* within the organization or project team is a key success factor. Contract in this context refers to a simple description or short agreement of what are required, when, dependencies and at what quality and cost. Having an established contract is not because of mistrust, it is about ensuring discipline to get work done. Some stakeholders may not want to have any signed commitment or agreement in order to avoid being regularly monitored and held accountable or responsible for specific deliverables.

- *Good attitudes, friendly and service oriented organization* are vital to the successful management of service life cycle. A service oriented organization organizes people and teams around services. That is, it makes service outcome the driver for the organization structure. In a service oriented organization every resource recognizes that he/she is playing a role, regardless of the job title; job specification should be generic to some extent in order to provide latitude.

- To manage project successfully, *focus on the deliverables and outcome*; rely on the combination of your knowledge, experience and capable others to get the work planned and executed. From the onset, *promote team maturity through the project team values* which should guide the conduct of the project team activities.

- *Always have the end in mind and do the first thing first*. This will prevent forth and back movements, and it enables you to save valuable time and money.

Complementary Practices

Complementary practices are practices that complement each other or make other practices effective. Good project management practices require supporting practices like effective governance, leadership commitment and discipline. An organization with effective governance, leadership discipline and passion for service excellence facilitates and promotes effective service life cycle management.

Effective project management and product delivery management practices yield high benefits to the organization, leading to maturity and provides the necessary feedback to the organization strategy development. A good practice does not work or become effective in isolation. Understanding the effect of complementary practices will enable organizations to detect point of failure of practices and ensure that complementary practices are established to ensure project delivery success.

For example, if project charter is a mandatory project management artifact, to ensure its credibility and sustenance, the responsible stakeholders must have the discipline to spend quality time to review and approve it, and commit to implementing the charter content. Also, if an organization requires realistic progress tracking and status reporting, it must commit itself to realistic planning and schedule, which are base-lined on realistic expectations and commensurate resource capacity.

Blank page

Part 4: Project Management

This part describes the project management processes and key skills required to successfully deliver a project. It includes the following topics:

- Project Management Life Cycle - Generic Frameworks
- Project Management Life Cycle - Practical Project Management Approach
- Key Success Skills - Functional
- Key Success Skills - Soft
- Key Success Skills - Financial
- Key Success Skills - Other

Blank page

Chapter 13 - Project Management Life Cycle

Effective use of project management processes, techniques, tools and resources (people, materials, equipment and money) facilitate successful delivery of projects.

Generic Frameworks

The current de facto project management methodologies are the PMI® (Project Management Institute) PMBOK® and PRINCE® (PRojects IN Controlled Environments, currently PRINCE2®). There are other variations and customized versions from different organizations. However, the most popular and widely adopted is the PMI® methodology, referred to as PMBOK®.

PMI Methodology - An Overview

Project Management Institute (PMI®) developed the Project Management Body of Knowledge (PMBOK®) as a general guide for managing projects. PMBOK® includes five process groups and nine knowledge areas, combined to facilitate structured approach to project management. Figure 12 is a representation of the PMBOK® methodology. It shows the key elements and their overlapping dependencies. The overlaps shown are not exact but realistic timing and dependencies of the key elements. It includes the following:

- Five process groups - Initiating, Planning, Executing, Controlling and Monitoring, and Closing.

- Nine knowledge areas - Project Integration Management, Project Scope Management, Project Time Management, Project Cost Management, Project Quality Management, Project Human Resource Management, Project Communication Management, Project Issue/Risk Management and Project Procurement Management.

Each process group and knowledge area consists of sub-processes and work packages, which are represented by inputs, tools and techniques, and outputs. The knowledge areas and the processes or sub-processes within them are applied to and fall within one or more of the five process groups.

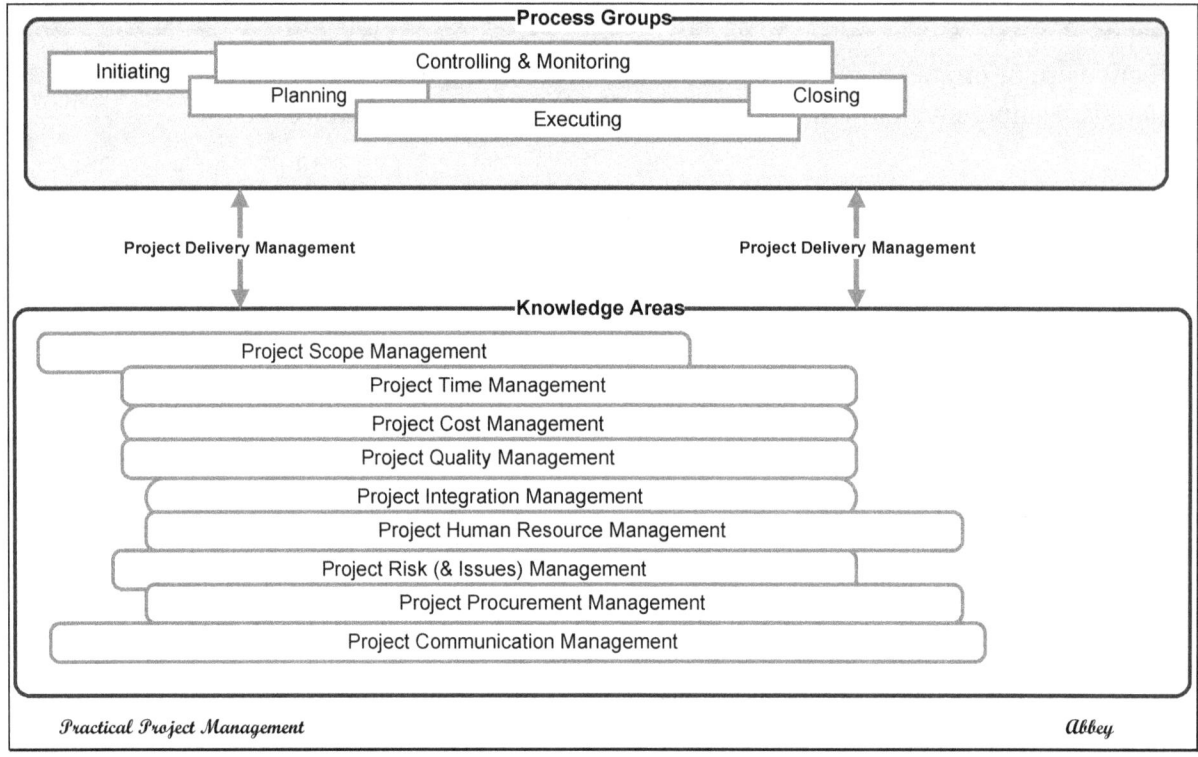

Figure 12 - Project Management Institute® Methodology

Prince2 Methodology - An Overview

PRojects IN Controlled Environments (PRINCE2®), second major version, is a project management method, which includes the organization, management and control of a project. PRINCE2 is a registered trademark of the Office of Government Commerce (OGC), United Kingdom.

PRINCE2 established 45 sub-processes categorized into eight processes:

- Starting Up a Project (SU)

- Planning (PL)

- Initiating a Project (IP)

- Directing a Project (DP)

- Controlling a Stage (CS)

- Managing Product Delivery (MP)

- Managing Stage Boundaries (SB)

- Closing a Project (CP)

PMBOK® and PRINCE2® are the most popular generic project management methodologies. Organizations tend to stick to a preferred method that they are used to and work for them. The purpose of this discussion is not to go into debate about which method is preferred, but to recognize the existence of structured project management methodologies and their contributions to delivering projects successfully.

It is very important to know that projects are unique endeavours, and the blind application of a generic methodology (PMBOK® or PRINCE2®) may not produce the desired result. Considering the generic nature of these methodologies, organizations have customized versions to manage industry specific projects.

Even the use of the customized industry version or a part of it may need to be adapted to the specific need of each project, on a case by case basis. The main goal is to identify and apply a fit-for-purpose method to accomplish the desired result. This requires skills, experience, maturity and commitment of the business and project management professionals. It takes good practices, for organizations and professionals, to mature.

Figure 13 shows the representation of the PRINCE2® methodology.

Going forward, the practical approach to project management, through the effective application of the generic methodologies, techniques and tools, and good practices, will be discussed.

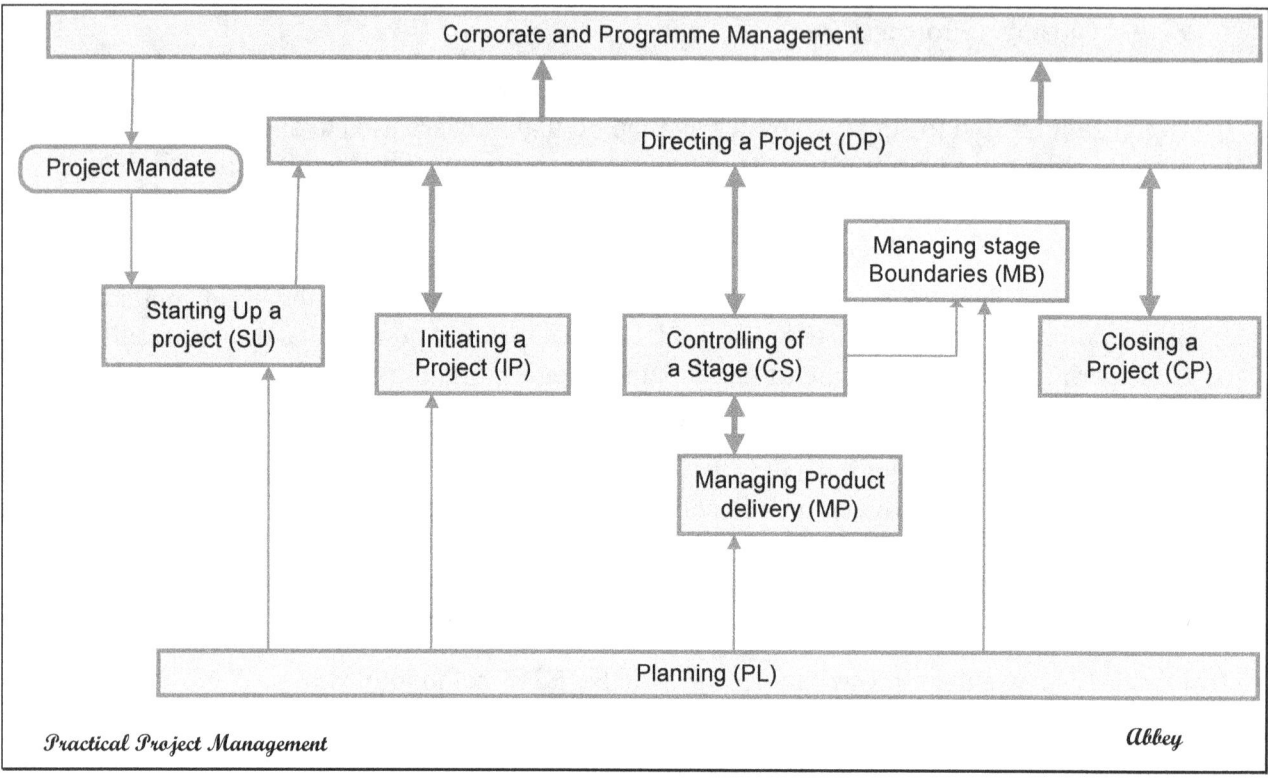

Figure 13 - PRINCE2® Methodology

Practical Project Management Approach

Practical project management is accomplished through effective application of good practices, using fit-for-purpose processes, techniques and tools. The practical project management processes are customized version of the generic industry frameworks, with creative elements that create value. Some organizations have customized methodology, which specify mandatory and optional deliverables or artifacts. The flexibility of the methodology should promote creativity without compromising the consistent use of the processes, techniques and tools. Consistency ensures effective team interaction and successful projects delivery.

Sole reliance on processes, techniques and tools may fall short of delivering projects successfully except they are consistently used in a disciplined way through good practices. Good practices require discipline and commitment of the stakeholders in order to provide, effectively manage and use project information. Every aspect must demonstrate value through the relevance of the project information and results. It is important to focus on relevant information because stakeholders will only pay attention to what they considered valuable.

Figure 14 shows a practical project management methodology framework. It shows the gating and supporting processes for project management and product delivery management, and the interactions between them. This framework fits within the service life cycle (discussed in chapter 10). It establishes clear dependency and scope for project management and product delivery management process groups.

For small projects (definition depends on the organization, for example a project between 30 to 90 days delivery window), some gates, steps and deliverables could be omitted or waived, compressed or consolidated to ensure quick and timely delivery, without compromising key project delivery discipline and good practices. This is organization dependent. For example, a simple term of reference may suffice for project charter and plan, and the governance approvals may be less strict.

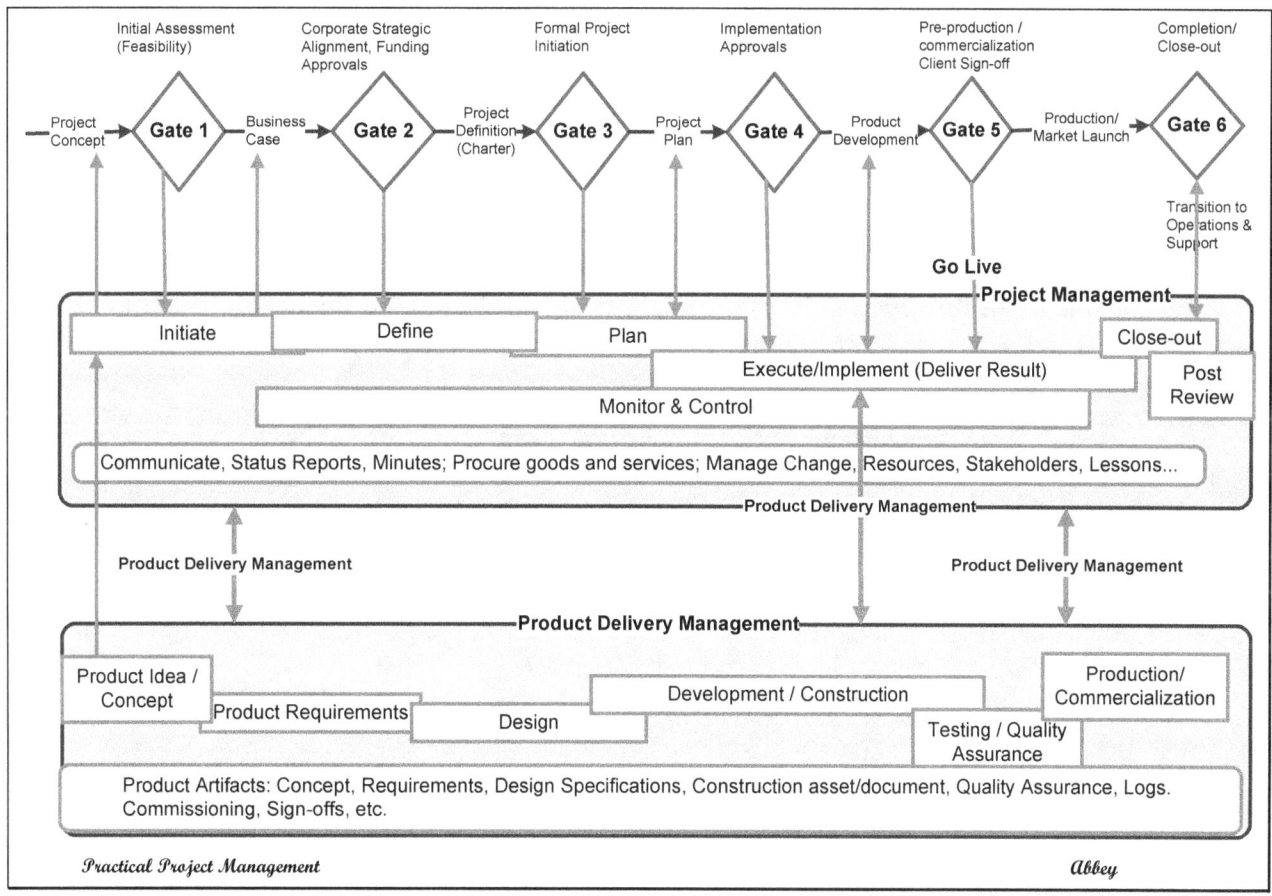

Figure 14 - A Practical Project Management Methodology

Chapter 14 - Key Success Skills

"People are always blaming their circumstances for what they are. I don't believe in circumstances. The people who get on in this world are the people who get up and look for the circumstances they want, and, if they can't find them, make them."

George Bernard Shaw

All the attributes and skills described here are specialized disciplines. There are specialized training in each of these key skills, which you may take or may have taken as part of your career development. However, the goal here is to provide succinct descriptions and the importance of their applications when you are in the field.

The purpose of the key success skills section is to provide concise, well thought out and practical guide on what they are, tips, hints and their practical applications, which combined to make you a seasoned, smarter, more thoughtful and successful project (and/or business) manager. To creatively and successfully apply these skills you need understanding, courage and sound judgment. ***Fear could turn your intelligence into mediocrity***.

These skills are grouped into functional, financial, soft and other skills. The positioning of each skill within a group is debatable. For instance, financial category was separated from the others, due to the diligence and serious importance attached to the financial aspect of a project. The key is to understand these skills and their importance to the success of your project(s).

Chapter 15 - Key Success Skills – Functional

Communication

"Weakness of attitude becomes weakness of character."   *Albert Einstein*

It is a widely published and known fact that 90% of a project manager's time should be or is spent on communication. Communication includes several activities (meetings, managing conflicts, discussions, debates, reporting etc.) conducted by different means (e- mail, phone, fax, teleconference, video conference etc.) at different times and places. Though communication involves multiple parties, the project manager should take responsibility for clear understanding of all messages between parties involved in a project, thus ensuring smooth information flow.

Communication is about sending and receiving clear and specific messages that are understood by the parties involved. These messages translate into desirable actions and outcome. Communication can be direct and/or interactive through verbal, signs and body language. In interactive communication the preferred mode is constructive discussion. Constructive discussion leads to solutions, while destructive discussion leads to deadlock.

Communication Techniques

"Writing without thinking is like shooting without aiming."   *Arnold Glasgow*

Before you initiate a communication identify appropriate audience or recipients of the message, and ensure that the theme, subject or agenda is stated clearly to encourage focused message and discussion. That does not entirely prevent distractions caused by others who may not share the theme or intentionally and silently pursuing a different agenda. However, stating your theme, subject or agenda upfront enables you to focus or re-focus the participants on the message.

Effective communication requires maturity, understanding, professionalism and good judgement. A project manager should have a big heart, not focusing on noises or distractions. Your ability to recognize trees from the forest, differentiate reality from fiction, deception and politics from straight talk, and diplomacy from misrepresentation, will play a big role in crafting your message and response to every situation. As a project manager, you should be sensitive, bold and decisive; be tolerant of diverse opinions but not tolerant of non-performance, which could negatively affect team effort and project outcome.

You may be distracted, dealing with difficult people, insulted and rudely treated by a stakeholder. However, your ability to maturely resist distractions and not give in to cheap shots will be rewarding. Recognizing every bad or ugly situation and its impact on the outcome will help you to determine the right judgement to ensure positive outcome.

The use of a well established project governance and communication plan will enhance your communication effectiveness. A communication plan should at the minimum identify and specify key stakeholders, their interests, message description, message format and frequency. A clear communication plan captures stakeholders' expectations and ensures that relevant messages are shared with the appropriate stakeholders.

Obtain the communication requirements from all stakeholders, to develop the communication plan. Validate the communication plan with the stakeholders, that is, obtain their consent. Table 1 contains a reference or link to a communication plan/guide template.

Table 1 - Communication Guide Template

PPMBook\ProjectManagement\PPM_CommunicationPlan.doc

Communication Hints and Tips

- ***Do not in any way misrepresent or manipulate facts***. You may get immediate benefits, but the end result and consequences may be more costly than the earlier gains. Be factual and tactful.

- ***Do not allow your ego to be paramount in dealing with others and project issues***. You have to be focused; you cannot afford not to be. Many things happen on projects - good, bad and ugly. Your ability to stay above the water will always pay off to making the project successful.

- ***Avoid sending generic messages or reports***. Send customized, focused and relevant messages to the stakeholders. Some stakeholders may consider your message irrelevant (this may not be necessarily true) due to non-direct value to their specific role or due to frustration in dealing with the high volume of messages they receive. Do not take it personal. You may not be able to please everyone, just fine tune your communication approach and information sharing effectiveness, based on the circumstance. ***Limit the number of messages and reports you send out or publish***. Keep it simple, consolidate where possible and share with the relevant recipients.

- ***Avoid resolving conflict via e-mail or fax***, as they may be recorded, recalled or referenced for purposes you may not expect. Preferred and recommended method is face-to-face discussion. Explore other verbal means where face-to-face meeting is not possible, especially in the case of remote teams.

- ***Whatever you do, show good attitudes and behaviours.*** These are what people see. Keep your personal and cultural believes to yourself, they may impact your attitude and behaviours. No matter what you do, not everyone will be pleased, because some may make a perception of you even without knowing you well enough. It takes time to build trust and you may not have enough time to do that during the duration of a typical project. However, your effort, candour and accomplished result will be the evidence of your substance.

- ***Showing good attitudes should be a given for a project manager***. Realising you may not always be right, acknowledge your mistakes and you will not drag issues unnecessarily. Most stakeholders will show understanding if you acknowledge your mistakes and demonstrate ability to learn fast. Nonetheless given in, in order to smooth things over or hide issues, is not advisable. There are situations where compromise could make sense, for instance when there is no apparent difference in value creation from alternate options. You are not a project manager because you are smarter than others, it is a discipline or role that you have chosen to make a difference, so act wisely.

- ***Do not expect everyone to agree with everything you say or do.*** Ensure you have the buy-in of most stakeholders. However, if you have to wait until everyone agrees with your message or proposal, you may never accomplish anything. Sometimes it is wise to act first and ask for forgiveness later.

- ***Be respectful, show good manners, and act fairly and legally***. Good behaviours are not constraint by believes or cultures, rather they cut across cultural boundaries. These behaviours will take you anywhere and enable you to connect with your project teams, even in a multi-cultural setting or organization.

- ***Be aware of others egos, ask questions rather than dictate***. This will enable you to elicit facts and bring out the best in others. Whatever you do, be patient but act swiftly. There are differences between patience and slackness, and between swiftness and erratic behaviour.

- ***The quality of the matching of your words, actions and result is the measure and evidence of your substance and performance***.

- ***When you have a meeting or presentation, particularly with the external stakeholders, spend time to prepare with the core team and other key stakeholders*** to clarify agenda, capture issues, review options and understand implications of the situations. This way you minimize surprises during the actual meeting or presentation.

- ***Promote interactive meetings and presentations***. This way, stakeholders feel a sense of belonging, participation and responsibility for the information being shared and decision making, going forward. This in turn promotes commitment to fulfil stakeholders' expectations.

- ***When you communicate with the business clients avoid the use of technical or professional jargons***. Shield them away from the product technicalities and express every situation in terms of solutions, issues/risks management and value creation.

Presentation

Presentation is a major part of communication activities. Each presentation should be focused to the target audience. The key steps to effective presentation include the following:

- **Define the subject of discussion**, the goal of the presentation and the audience.

- **Plan your agenda**. Outline, gather and prepare content and practice before the presentation.

- **Ensure a clear path from start to end**, make the connection. Focus on the key issues and avoid fluffy stuff.

- **Be comfortable and sound natural**, and stick to the relevant points and keep to time. Be simple, clear and audible.

- **Listen attentively and respond to criticism gracefully** or turn criticism into opportunities.

- **Make it interactive**, particularly if you are seeking suggestions and/or decision on the next steps.

- **Re-state objectives** at the beginning and at the end; confirm understanding and positions of the audience. Include details and additional information, if applicable, in the attachment or as appendix.

Scope Management

"The difference between genius and stupidity is that genius has limits."   **Albert Einstein**

To be a successful project manager, you must ensure and maintain a clear, accurate and concise scope for the project, regardless of the changes during the life time of the project. That is, include only the required work or specific requirements to fulfill the project goals. Otherwise, some stakeholders may exploit situations where scope is not properly managed and controlled. Usually most people continue certain behaviours as long as they are getting result. Handle each scope change request based on its own merit and demonstrate the implications of the change to the client to aid in making appropriate decisions.

A competent project manager understands (or seeks to understand) the project mandate, goal and expected outcome, and is able to explain them to the project team and other stakeholders. The project mandate is a point of reference to ensure and sustain project team focus. Run-away projects occur due to lack of controllable scope, caused by 'scope creep' (i.e. uncontrolled introduction of new request into an active project). Scope creep should be controlled through effective scope change management.

It is very important to include scope change management procedure in the project charter and integrated project plan to remind the client of the importance of respecting the original scope and following due process to effect scope change. This does not have to be an elaborate procedure to ensure its effectiveness; however, it should be clear in terms of the key steps, roles and responsibilities. Emphasizing the importance of scope change management and the implications of disrespecting it should be discussed, as required, with the client and other key stakeholders.

Avoid making significant scope change (or any change, if possible) towards the later part of the project life cycle, to prevent delay to the project completion. The change management workflow is described in Chapter 24 - Monitoring and Controlling. Table 2 includes a reference or link to a scope management document template.

Table 2 - Scope Management document template

> Template: PPMBook\ProjectManagement\PPM_ScopeManagement.doc

Problem Solving

"We can't solve problems by using the same kind of thinking we used when we created them."
                                                                                        Albert Einstein

Effective problem solving, at every stage of the project life cycle, is critical to the successful delivery of projects. Simplifying or breaking down sometimes seemingly complex issue is at the heart of problem solving. The project management itself is about developing solution to a major problem, for example, constructing a new road to promote trade between cities, delivering a modernize health operation equipment to reduce surgery turn-around time etc.

Problem Solving Technique

Sometimes it is a wise idea to involve external parties, not originally part of the project team, in solving problems. This provides independent thoughts and expertise in problem analysis, diagnosis and resolution.

Solving problems require the following **key steps**:

- *Problem profile:* includes problem name, owner, stakeholders and roles. Log the problem as an issue or risk to be resolved.

- *Problem definition and description:* guides the problem understanding, analysis and resolution.

- *Investigation, analysis and diagnosis:* brainstorm ideas, identify root causes, divide and conquer (break down into smaller parts), and propose solution options or alternatives. In doing this, separate ideas generation or options identification from ideas evaluation to ensure that several alternatives are considered towards establishing an optimized solution.

- *Test solution options:* subject the solution options to quality testing and recommend or choose an optimized solution.

- *Implement solution* and verify resolution.

- *Close:* document the problem, solution and lessons learnt.

Time and Priority Management

"You will never find time for anything, if you want time you must create it."Charles Buxton

Time is money, it is fixed. Realistically, you have only 24 hours per day, 7 days a week, 365 days a year (except leap year - 365 plus ¾ day). You have the choice and opportunity to allocate and use your time as you wish. You cannot stress the time; you can only explore it wisely.

Do not delude yourself about multi-tasking, except you are a multi-person or engage several persons to work on some tasks in parallel, where and when possible. In computing, the concept of time slicing, with single processor, was called multi-tasking; however, real multi-tasking was achieved through multi-processors. In essence what most people called multi-tasking is juggling multiple tasks, using time slicing. Time slicing re-allocates a processor time to a newly active task while a previously active task is temporarily inactive or idle.

The way you use your time makes a significant difference to your life and the result you accomplish. Remember the ***80:20 rules***. It has many plausible interpretations. For example, 20% of productive people's time is spent adding 80% value to total productivity. It means most people spend 80% of the time on things that add little or no value. Hence the difference between great outcome and just okay outcome could be the effective management of the same time available to all of us.

Know your limit. Considering the effect of the law of diminishing returns, working long hours does not usually correlate to delivering more. Knowing and keeping to your optimal functioning limit promotes good health, alertness and effectiveness in delivering successful and quality outcomes. Healthy workforce is a highly productive workforce.

It does not matter how busy you are, the important thing is what you are busy doing. Spending most of your time doing quality and valuable things that help push the limit is very critical to the success of your outcome. Hypocrisy and mediocrity are two things that you have to deal with, as a project manager or leader, by assigning well defined work packages or activities, with agreed quality, time and cost, and ensuring timely feedback on show stoppers. You have to be on your guard and take nothing for granted.

The key to effective time management is not just about techniques and tools, it is about practice, practice and practice. ***Prioritize effectively***; eliminate tasks that add no value. Aim before you shoot. ***Practice delete, defer, delegate and act***. Whenever you have a new action item, you should decide whether to act on it now, defer it, delegate it, delete or keep it for information only.

Table 3 shows a sample time/priority management matrix. Time/priority management matrix enables you to manage your daily, weekly, monthly, quarterly and yearly priorities in a way that enables you to focus on the first thing first. The goal is to focus your attention on current and top priorities, track and monitor their status.

Table 3 - Time/Priority Management Matrix

Timing – March, 2009		
(Daily, Weekly, Monthly etc.)		
H (Urgency ↑)	• Documents re-organization – complete items clean-up	• Enterprise Financial System project – Complete project charter • Interactive Voice Recognition project – Decommission old system • Practical PM book project – Complete agenda outline
	• Reading/Study: Mastering strategy • Future vacation plans	• Status reports – all projects • Ab9.NET – complete site design • Personal – complete physical check-up
L	L...Importance →..	

Note:
The items in the boxes may include project work packages, activities and tasks, and other work activities. Customize the matrix for your specific needs. Be realistic – limit each box to 3 items. Priority groups include
1. High-Importance / High-Urgency (requires most attention)
2. High-Importance / Low-Urgency
3. Low-Importance / High-Urgency
4. Low-Importance / Low-Urgency (least attention, mostly deferred items)

PPMBook\ProjectManagement\PPM_TimePriorityManagment.doc

Research - Fact Finding

Research skills could be applied to small, medium and large undertakings and may span short to long time to complete. The goal is to explore and come up with a solution to a problem or situation.

Key steps to a successful research include:

- Identify and describe the key issues that need to be addressed.

- Define and establish the research objectives. These objectives are critical to the success of the research outcome.

- Determine data/information sources and types.

- Determine research approach (qualitative and/or quantitative).

- Design the research method (data gathering, study, survey etc.).

- Collect/gather the required data.

- Analyze data.

- Report outcome.

Each step must be handled with due diligence to avoid research errors and avoid faulty or inaccurate outcome reporting. Research goal is to report the fact, not working from the answer to the question.

Conflict Resolution

"In critical and baffling situations, it is always best to return to first principle and simple action."
Winston Churchill

Some people may believe that conflict is bad for the project team and try to avoid or hide them. Practically and to the contrary, conflict could be good for the team, be it personal or professional. It brings to the open the hidden issues, which if not discussed and resolved, could have devastating implications for the project.

Conflicts could take different forms. In projects, the most common conflict categories are personal and professional. All conflicts, be it personal (could be due to personal ego or personality clash) or professional (due to differed opinions or ideas), need to be confronted and addressed timely and decisively, before rumours and misinformation take control over the facts.

In a personal conflict, two or more team members may have past grudges which could affect their relationships and conducts on the project. For a professional conflict, there could be strong debate on alternate solutions being passionately and aggressively pursued by individuals or groups within the project team. Personal conflicts may take longer time to resolve than the professional conflict. One of the reasons is the fact that personal conflict causes are usually hidden and may take longer time to discover. In project management, conflicts can be resolved through negotiation, instruction, arbitration and diplomacy, among other techniques.

Tip to remember: Avoid resolving conflict via e-mail and fax, as they may be recorded, recalled or referenced inappropriately and used in ways you never anticipated. Preferred conflict resolution method is face-to-face discussion, combining effective and honest communication, counselling and negotiation or mediation.

In resolving conflicts, adopt or encourage debate rather than argument. Debate or respectful discussion leads to agreement (win-win outcome). Argument or destructive discussion leads to deadlock (loose-loose outcome) or mediocre solution (win-loose or loose-win outcome) at best. When you move from debate about issues to proposal of options or solutions to resolve identified issues, further discussions of the options lead to acceptable resolution, albeit not completely sometimes but could lead to shift in previously rigid positions. Debate approach shows that fair and honest resolution is desired, and it, usually, encourages the parties involved to co-operatively work together to resolve conflicts.

Depending on the nature of the conflict, you may have to resort to other conflict resolution methods such as dictate based on positional power (usually the last resort, but not recommended) or instruct, particularly in a situation whereby the cost of doing nothing outweigh the viable conflict resolution method.

Issues and Risks Management

Risk management is a discipline of identifying, assessing, mitigating and monitoring risks. Issues management is concerned with identifying, assessing, resolving and monitoring issues. Note the difference - risk mitigation and issue resolution. An issue is a potential problem that needs to be resolved now or as soon as possible in order to prevent negative impact on the project. A risk is a form of issue, which can be avoided or mitigated (by direct action, or indirect action - e.g. insurance). Risk can be expressed qualitatively (descriptive - e.g. emotional stress leading to lower moral and low performance) and quantitatively (measured in numeric term - e.g. loss of profit due to anticipated competitors' strategic action).

Risk is measured as: (probability or likelihood of an event occurring)*(impact of the event occurring). Risks can be categorized into financial, political, technology, project management, organization, environment and business risks.

- Issues and risks can, and should, be identified at any point in the project life cycle. The project team members should work together to identify risks and act responsibly to mitigate, eliminate or minimize their impact.

- Issues and risks profile and tracking should include: identity (short description), likelihood, impact, date identified, action parties, target resolution date, status monitoring and outcome.

- Issues and risks should be logged for tracking, monitoring and future references, as part of the knowledge base or historical information. They should be part of the project team meeting agenda, not only as and when they occur or an ad-hoc event - being proactive is the key here.

Table 4 includes a reference or link to issues and risks management document template.

Table 4 - Issues & Risks Management Template

PPMBook\ProjectManagement\PPM_IssuesRisksManagement.doc

Product/Industry Experience

The project manager does not have to be the product/industry subject matter expert, but requires good understanding or knowledge of the industry and/or product of the project; some past experience will be highly desirable. This will help the project manager to ask relevant questions, coordinate better, understand and respond to issues faster and engage the team in a timely and effective way.

Some level of understanding or knowledge of the product/industry is very valuable, sometimes necessary, for successfully delivery of projects. The product subject matter expert is usually responsible for the product delivery management or a sub-set of it.

Examples of product/industry include engineering (electrical, mechanical, civil, chemical, and architecture), information technology, accounting/finance, human capital management among others and their specialized areas such as road construction, power engineering, computer software, data management, commercial banking, pharmaceuticals etc.

Procurement/Contract Management

Projects make use of resources (professionals, equipment, materials and services) to accomplish their goals. Some resources could be internal to the organization or already available, while others could be external to the organization. External resources are procured through contracts/agreements, offered by the receiving (demanding and paying) organization and accepted by the supplying organization.

The focus here is the procurement of external resources for the project. However, the same procurement processes (as-is or modified) could be used to secure internal resources, particularly in large organizations where resources are shared through cost sharing or established internal processes and agreements.

Figure 15 shows the procurement key phases and steps. Each organization may have its own customized and detailed processes for each phase. The important thing is to understand the phases and steps, which make up the procurement life cycle and the critical elements to ensure a smooth flow end-to-end.

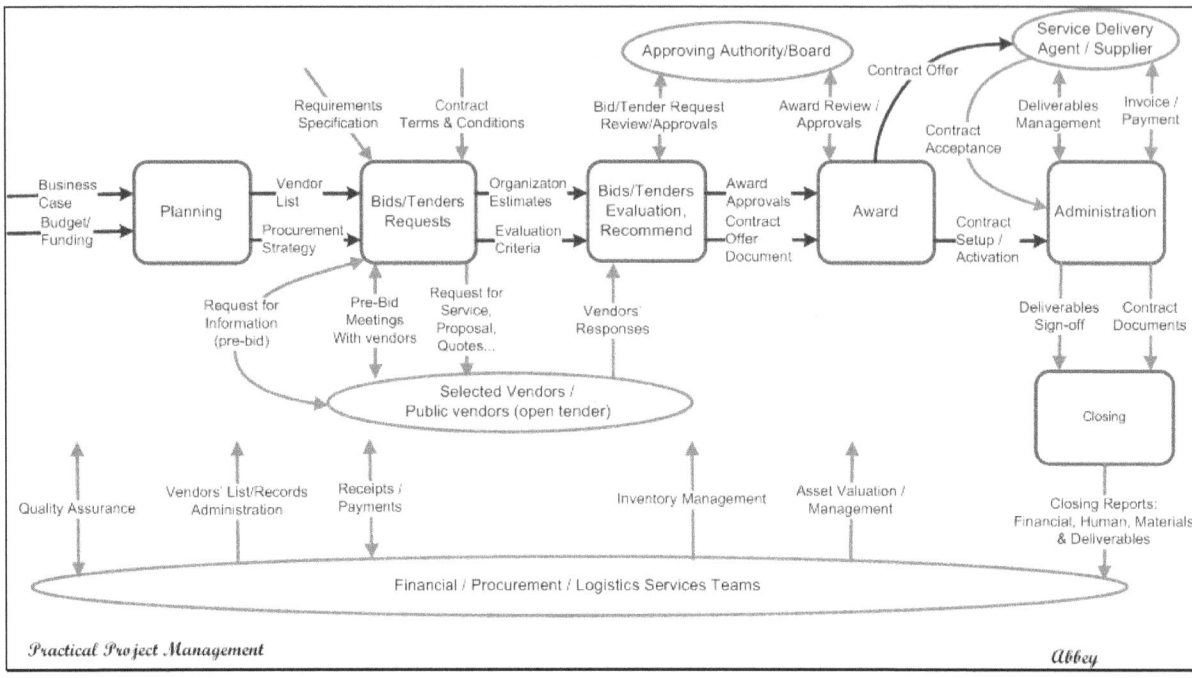

Figure 15 - Procurement Guide

Stakeholders Relationship Management

Dealing effectively with the stakeholders within and outside your core project team is crucial to the success of your project. Stakeholders include client representatives, sponsor(s), champion, business and technology subject matter experts, project team members, suppliers, service providers and agents. In the course of the project life cycle, you will deal with various stakeholders using written or formal contracts and, sometimes, informal agreements.

Your communication, contract/procurement management, negotiation and influencing skills will serve you well here. Particularly when you deal with suppliers, you need to have good grasp of the suppliers' contractual obligations and ensure that they are respected and followed. Whatever you do, do it professionally and legally. Avoid conflict of interest or principal-agent problem, which could compromise your good judgement or lead to a biased judgement.

Either separately or as part of the communication management plan, maintain a human resource availability chart and contact information for the project stakeholders. This will enable you to know who is available when and possible backup person to ensure continuity of planned activities and accommodate their absences in your project schedule.

In addition to maintaining up-to-date stakeholders' contact and roles information, it is useful to maintain **stakeholders' influence assessment,** represented by a **power-influence matrix**. Table 5 shows the stakeholders' power-influence matrix. Keep this confidential to yourself. You do not want to let stakeholders know your perception of their power and influence, which could vary depending on the aspect of the project management activities under consideration.

The power-influence matrix could be created and customized per project, per process group, per work package or per deliverable, to make it specific and effective. Understanding the influence and impact of the stakeholders on the project enables you to anticipate and prepare to manage challenges and ensure successful desired outcome.

Take note of the following in managing the project stakeholders:

- The importance of *timely engagement of stakeholders* cannot be understated, as it goes a long way to obtaining valuable support and commitment of others. Avoid after-thought involvement of the key stakeholders; though *better be late than never* could be your last rule of engagement.

- *Be self-aware and pay attention to projects and other activities*, which your project depends upon to be successful. However, *mind your business* and avoid being engrossed or distracted by events or activities that are not related to your project.

- You may interact with overzealous stakeholders whose actions, like trying to play the project manager's role, may affect project team dynamics and outcome. You need to continuously *educate your stakeholders about the need to work in harmony* for the good of the project. This may seem obvious, but it pays to discuss and re-emphasise the need for cooperation and its implications for the project. *You are the captain of the ship and accountable for safe sailing.* Even if the President is in the ship or on board, he/she can make demands (needs, change request etc.), but he/she should not tell you how to sail the ship, to ensure safe voyage. If you are not in control of the ship, you cannot make excuse for failing to remain a competent captain in turbulent waters. Therefore, *stay focussed and sail safely as a bold, courageous and competent captain*.

Table 5 - Stakeholders Power-Influence Matrix

Stakeholders Power-Influence Matrix		
H	• A. Lev, Service Delivery Manager	• John Paul, Project Sponsor • Azu Azoh, System Delivery Engineer • •
Power/Authority ↑	• Binta Lee, Project Analyst • Dave Zo, QA Analyst	• Project Champion • Ade John, Technical Lead - Infrastructure Design •
L	L..Influence →	

Note:
The information above are samples only, and the names used are fictitious (not real). This could be created or customized per phase, per work package, per deliverable etc.
1.   High-Power / High-Influence (highest impact, requires most attention)
2.   High- Power / Low- Influence
3.   High- Power / Low- Influence
4.   Low- Power / Low- Influence (least impact)
Keep this confidential to yourself. You do not want to let the stakeholders know your perception of their power and influence (which could vary depending on the aspect of the project management activities under considerations).

PPMBook\ProjectManagement\PPM_SRMInfluence.doc

Human Capital Management

"Given a choice, most people will opt to succeed. They will surprise you with their resourcefulness and determination. All they need is some help with their technique and a little encouragement from a mentor."   *James A. Hatherley*

As a project manager, out of everything you manage, either directly or indirectly, the most delicate and important part is the human capital management. Depending on your organization structure and culture, you may or may not have direct positional power over your team members. Your professional maturity, effective communication, influencing and negotiation skills are very crucial, particularly with stakeholders you do not have direct control over.

The key here is effective communication. It requires maturity, understanding, professionalism and good judgement. A project manager should be sensitive, bold and decisive; tolerant of diverse opinions, but not tolerant of non-performance, which could negatively affect team effort and project outcome. What you need is a committed, not conforming, team to achieve success. Deal cautiously and fairly with the project team members. Wrongful use of power makes people to be mediocre or conformant. Table 3 - Time/Priority Management Matrix (page 68) is applicable to human capital management.

As a project manager, you may experience strange and unprofessional behaviours from some stakeholders, within and outside the core project team. These are part of the challenges that confront a project manager. Ensure that you do not allow such behaviours to derail the success of the project. Focus your attention on results and deal appropriately with the behaviours that impact them. You may ignore, respond maturely or defer your response and avoid noises to ensure that you accomplish the desired outcome. It is not strange, but the situation could be tempting to fall for it, so beware and do not allow others' behaviours to derail the success of your project. You will not regret acting wisely.

Team building is a key aspect of effective human capital management. Take note of the following, as part your team building effort.

- ***Promote, among your team, shared vision, shared responsibility or work sharing***. Avoid the blame game, and encourage team members to take leadership role on assigned work package, activities or tasks.

- ***Leadership***: Encourage and promote leadership behaviours in your team. Each person responsible for the delivery of an assigned work package, activity or task is a leader in his/her own capacity and responsible for seeking others support to successfully complete the assigned work. Leadership cut across different levels and effective leadership effort coordination produces top result, by engaging everyone and creating a sense of belonging.

- ***Sometimes people could be the problem***. However, you may not be able to solve all people's problems. Those that are interpersonal among team members should be your focus. A long time personal issue which has become endemic in a person attitude and behaviours are difficult and usually takes time to resolve. What is your best way out? Encourage professionalism by ensuring each team member understand his/her role as an actor in the current '*episode*' (project) as transient and accept the contractual obligation to act in accordance to the contract terms, as their roles may vary from project to project.

Monitoring and Controlling

"Trust but verify."   *Ronald Reagan*

In order to effectively monitor and control project activities, **work assignments should be clearly defined and measured**. Remember the simple rule: you cannot measure what you have not defined; you cannot monitor and control what you have not measured. Measure the relevant things in order to ensure the effectiveness of the monitoring and controlling activities. For instance, measuring how many hours someone spent in the office, per day or per week, may be of little use or less effective compared to measuring the quantity and quality of work completed within a time period.

Project manager should not leave things to chances. Trust your team but trust their deliverables more. Deliverable is the only thing that counts. "Trust but verify". You do not have to be a micro manager to monitor and control project activities. However, you need to set clearly defined work and expected outcome that the action parties understand in terms of the quality of the outcome, timing and cost. Monitoring key parameters and trends will serve as signals that will determine your next actions - drill down for more information, re-confirm expectations or adjust expectations. Essentially, you want to monitor specific work outcomes, schedule and financial performance, and exercise necessary control or corrective actions as appropriate.

Some medium to large size projects may engage the service of a quality assurance analyst to document and track agreed work packages, activities and associated deliverables. The goal is to avoid delays on the critical path items (items on the longest path of the project) and ensure that project quality expectations are met.

Work Organization

The importance of your work organization cannot be understated. A disorganized or less organized project manager could be a problem to the project. Having information is good, but if you cannot easily find the information in a timely fashion, it is not a pleasant thing. Therefore get organized. It is not difficult; rather it is more unpleasant to be disorganized. Effective organization of your work impacts your thought process and overall performance of your team and project. Essentially, you need to organise project vital information, including documentation, electronic mails and other materials (printed memos, faxes, contracts or agreements etc.). Figure 16 is a simplified structure for organizing your electronic mails and documentation. It can be customized based on your needs.

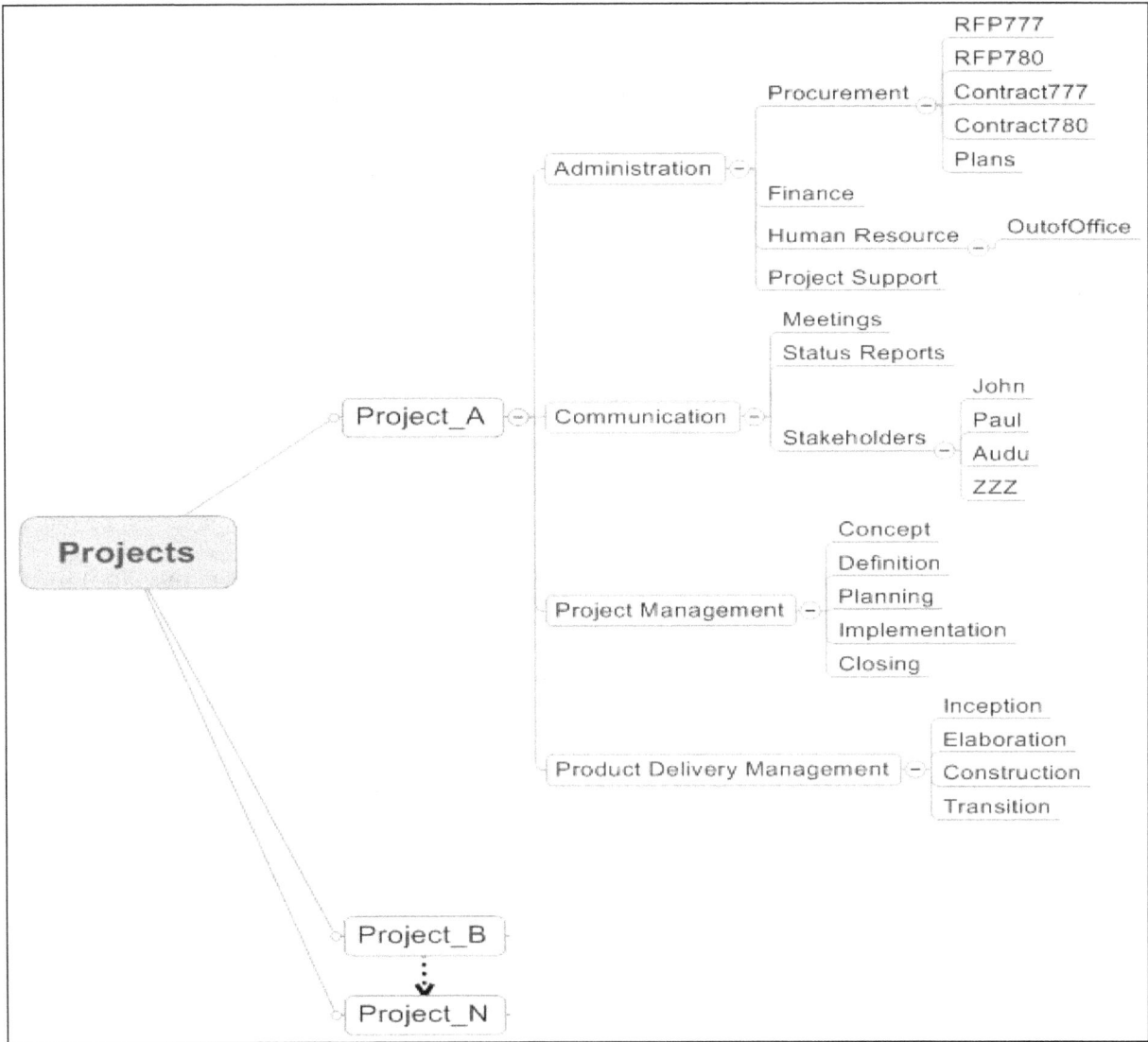

Figure 16 - Project (Work) Organization

Negotiation

Negotiation is one of the decision making techniques such as direct, instruct, arbitrate or mediate. Negotiation is the preferred decision making technique in situations where the parties involved do not have the direct power or control to determine what the other party should do. For instance, the buyer has money and the seller has the product/service, neither can legally obtain what the other has without given up something in return. That does not mean they will end up with the same real value of what will be exchanged - that depends on the skills of the negotiators. However, to both parties the worth of what is received and what is given up is considered the same or at par.

Negotiation in good faith means that an agreement for exchange is reached based on the merits of the options proposed. That is, you do not reach an agreement by tricks and ploys such as threat, aggression, condescending behaviours etc.; but by decent and legal means.

The following four key phases are critical to a successful negotiation: preparation, debating, proposing and bargaining. The key steps in each phase are discussed next.

Prepare/Plan:

- Identify the negotiating parties' interests.

- Identify key issues that need to be resolved and tradables (exchangeable items) required to fulfill your interests.

- Rank the tradables in order of importance and (guess) estimate the same for the other party.

- Establish your entry point and exit point (the maximum tolerance level or value) for the identified tradables that will fulfill your interests.

- The priorities you established will become valuable tools in your negotiation process.

Debate:

- Discuss in good faith - you can be reasonable and firm without given in to others' tricks, ploys and hypes.

- Debates constructively, do not engage in destructive debate (argument). Debate leads to solution, argument leads to deadlock.

- Constructive debate behaviours include making neutral or non-offensive statements, asking questions instead of assertions and assumptions, give assurance (a demonstration of paying attention to others' concerns) and summarizing negotiating parties' point of views.

- Argumentative behaviours include irritation, assumptions and assertions, interruption, point scoring, attack and blame game, and threats.

Propose:

- Essentially, debate moves you to proposal. When you make a proposal to fulfil an interest, ensure that you make it conditional, using firm language, without committing yourself. Proposal is for consideration, it is not a bargain or agreement, but could lead to an agreement, if both parties agreed to it. Proposals move from being tentative to specific as you move towards the bargaining or agreement phase.

- Your condition or demand on other negotiating party could be vague or specific, and your offer must be vague, in order to avoid committing yourself. Express the condition before the offer. Examples: if you are prepared to pay $1500 (specific condition), I may consider selling a measurable part (vague offer) of the goods; If you are prepared to lease at a reasonable (vague condition) discount, I may (vague offer) be willing to review the duration (vague offer) of the contract.

- Also, when you receive a proposal, your response should follow the above conditional statements. Ask questions to clarify the proposals before you respond.

- Having gone through series of proposals, you may have to summarise them and ensure clarity between what you are getting and what you are giving up.

Bargain (Close):

- Bargaining is about reaching an agreement.

- In bargaining, both condition and offer must be specific. Examples include: if you pay $1500, I will deliver 10 pieces of the temperature measuring devices; if you lease the vehicle for $250 per month, covering use and regular maintenance, I will accept the 4 year lease contract. Bargaining makes proposal specific.

- Ensure that the condition statement comes before the offer. 'Yes' response to a bargain means agreement. 'No' response means deadlock or another round of debate and proposals.

- Effective bargaining leads to an agreement.

- Once you have an agreement, put it in writing and obtain both parties approvals/signatures to make it bidding on both parties. This way you will avoid counter offer and/or counter claims after an agreement has been reached.

Revive a Troubled Project

"In critical and baffling situations, it is always best to return to first principle and simple action."
Winston Churchill

Sometimes, a new project manager may be required to take over an existing project, which may have been in trouble for various reasons. You can revive a troubled project by going to the basics. Do not mend a rag, it will become worse. The preferred approach is to review and renew the project concept and planning.

The following are the key steps to taking over and reviving a troubled or existing project:

- Review the current status, by referencing the existing project documents (project charter, milestones timeline, project schedule, integrated project plan, issues and risks records, and financials).

- Discuss with the existing core project team to review the status, issues and risks, challenges and experiences. Brainstorm options for resolving the identified issues and moving forward.

- Interview and discuss with other key stakeholders (including senior management team) on their expectations, concerns and support.

- Prepare a position paper, indicating the current status, key issues and options for the project realization (or cancellation, if appropriate); and recommend the way forward to the appropriate governing body. The goal is to maximize value and profit or minimize losses.

- Depending on the outcome of the review and the approval received, you may have to re-activate or cancel the project with adequate closing documentation.

Quality Management

Quality Management (QM) includes quality control, quality assurance and quality improvement. Quality control is ensured by setting key thresholds for the measured attributes and managing expectations within the established thresholds. Quality assurance ensures that the outcomes or deliverables meet the defined and agreed client expectations and standards. Quality improvement takes inputs from quality control and quality assurance to develop and implement solutions to address deficiency or improvement needs. Any defect or issue detected requires resolution which may be simple or complex. Some improvements may be implemented during the current project life cycle, through change management process, or deferred to a later date.

Quality management activities are performed for project management and product delivery management, as good practices. All phases, work packages and deliverables should be monitored for quality assurance. Exercise appropriate quality control measures to manage performances outside the established tolerance range or thresholds.

For product delivery management, quality assurance is usually accomplished through comprehensive product testing in the laboratory (a less expensive option) by the product experts or testing group, or in the field (a more expensive option) by selected users or customers.

Project Interface and Dependency

A project may have interfaces and interdependencies with other projects, organizations, technologies and partners. It is important to understand the nature of these dependencies and their implications for your project. Collaborate with the affected stakeholders to manage these interdependencies.

Key project interdependency attributes to record and manage include:

- Interface type, projects involved, organization, technology etc.

- Interface description

- Relationship - formal or informal

- Expectations - deliverables

- When to deliver the expected deliverables

- Key contacts

- Status and remarks

Table 6 includes a reference or link to a project interface document template.

Table 6 - Project Interface Template

Template: PPMBook\ProjectManagement\PPM_ProjectInterface.doc

Project interface and dependency is discussed further in part 6 (Deliver Result).

Chapter 16 - Key Success Skills - Soft

Inspire the team

Your confidence and show of courage, particularly during tough times, will help the team to beat the fear of failure and summon courage to tackle hard problems and challenges. You can inspire the team by engaging them through your words, actions, expertise and result.

As a source of inspiration, you act as a counsellor, mentor, coach and supporter for your team members. As a project manager, you are like a General in the army who is facing a tough battle. Though he is burning and troubled inside, as a courageous leader of the troops, he has to show good/determined face and behaviours to continue to encourage the troops, even during challenging times.

Influence

You need the influencing skills to convince people you do not have power to instruct or directly negotiate with, through tactical engagement and interactions. There is no catch-all solution to influencing others. It is more of an art than science. It requires experience and practice, and should be adaptable to different situations. Key steps to successful influence include:

- Define and establish common goals and interests.

- Discuss or debate with the stakeholders to establish understanding of the goals and interests, and key issues that will address the identified interests.

- Understand other parties' concerns or point of views.

- Work towards a common and agreeable understanding to achieve the desired outcome.

- Document and clarify agreements; follow-up and be prepared to repeat the above steps to ensure clarity and demonstrate the value of cooperation to the target audience.

Resilience and Tenacity

Your potential to deliver result is limited by your imagination and how you defined yourself, not by what others think of you.

Disagreement today does not mean disagreement forever. It may mean that your target audience is not satisfied, does not fully understand, appreciate or is not convinced about your current proposal or position. It is rare for people to say 'no' to best solution that works to their advantage, meet their needs and maximize value for them.

Through resilience and tenacity, 'no' now can turn to 'yes', failure can turn to success, weakness can turn into strength and threat can turn into opportunity. When you meet obstacle to or rejection of your proposal, you may need to review, revise or re-develop your options and proposal, having paid due diligence to the concerns raised by your client.

Political Acuity

"Equations are more important to me, because politics is for the present, but an equation is something for eternity."   *Albert Einstein*

The most important thing here is the political awareness. You do not need to be a political figure or professional politician. However, you need to be aware of when, why and how politics are used in your organization, particularly those that are, most often than not, geared towards personal, rather than organizational, interests.

A project manager should be sensitive, bold and decisive, and tolerant of diverse opinions. He/she should wisely manage behaviours that may jeopardize the interest of the project and the organization. In dealing with political issues, take note of the following:

- *Be more professional than political*. Politics in organizations may involve the use of unfair or illegal means to get result, which are mostly beneficial to individuals. Such approach breeds rancour, vengeful attitudes and behaviours. Never underrate the intelligence and power of others, irrespective of their levels in the organization. What you need is a committed, not conforming, team to achieve result. Wrongful use of power makes people conformant or mediocre at best.

- *You need practice and experience to handle political situations*, due to the unique nature of each occurrence and issues involved. No amount of theory, though helpful, will solve political issues.

- *Make decision and take action once you can accept the consequences*. Remember that sometimes it makes sense to act now and ask for forgiveness later. It may be your best bet in certain situations where nothing seems to be moving or get done. Though this is not a license to indulge in silly behaviours. You still have to take calculated risk, which takes skills and requires sound judgement. It may be necessary for the project manager to secure some alliances when extreme measures have to be taken or extra ordinary decisions have to be made.

Leadership

"Every man who takes office in Washington either grows or swells, and when I give a man office, I watch him carefully to see whether he is growing or swelling."   *Woodrow Wilson*

There are leadership qualities you should be aware of and practice to be a successful project manager. Leadership is not only for those in the executive, higher management and supervisory positions, or entrepreneurs. It cuts across every level of the organization. *Leadership is about being accountable, taking charge of an assignment, helping others to succeed, having the right attitude and commitment to go above and beyond the call of duty.* Leadership discipline contributes significantly to becoming and sustaining a performing organization.

As a leader or project manager, your role is to simplify things (such as vision, mission, scope, and deliverables) to a point where every responsible party can clearly understand his/her assignments and commit to deliver them. You should be proactive in discovering issues and risks, with help from all reliable sources. Help the team by ensuring or creating a clear path from the goal setting to result, remove obstacles to performance and set the team members up for success.

A leader is not threatened by strong characters, but open to and tolerant of diverse opinions. A leader encourages, believes and promotes healthy and open debates, promotes and celebrates service excellence. *A leader is like the conductor of an orchestra*. He/she makes no sound or plays no instrument, but his/her actions facilitate the delivery of a masterpiece musical show by the team of talented musical instruments' handlers. The leader's actions usually match the outcome.

Decision Making

"I never worry about action, but only inaction."   *Winston Churchill*

You will always be making decisions about actions to be taken at every stage of the project. No matter the situation you encounter, you cannot afford to do nothing if you want the project to remain active and move forward. There is no room for inaction on a live project, when time is ticking and money is depleting.

Indecision is not an option. It is simply a sign of confusion or incompetence. Some may say indecision or inaction is an option; that is only true for the lame and the confused. If fear of repercussion is preventing you from taking action, seek and ask for help. There are willing folks within your team, unit or organization or other professional colleagues who will share their thoughts and get you out of the confusion and stalemate. You are never alone, except you keep yourself from others, who are willing to help.

For every decision you are about to make, obtain facts from reliable sources and understand the consequences to a reasonable degree. A decision method is dependent on the situation. Decision methods may include any or combinations of the following: negotiate, consult, instruct or direct, mediate etc. *Make a decision and take actions once you have understood and accepted the implications or consequences of the decision.*

Stress Management

Stress is a common thing in the workplace due to the nature of the workplace. Workplace stress contributors include high work demand, time and cost constraints, people and other issues. Reasonable stress level could be good to move you from the comfort zone to creativity zone. Excessive and constant stress is a problem.

Understanding causes of stress will enable you to exercise preventive measures to manage and minimise stress in your workplace or project team. *Causes of stress* include the following:

- *Unrealistic expectations* - putting great demand on teams, beyond their capability, in order to do more at lower cost and/or in less time.

- *Incompetence* - inability to confidently perform an assignment either due to wrong self-assessment or due to assignment of tasks that are not commensurate to the resource skill set or capability.

- *Lack of enough rest* - long hours' work, without enough rest to be in a state of mind and physique to withstand regular long hours of work, could be a recipe for disaster.

- *Disorganization* of self, information and team.

- *Organization culture and practices* - high level of bureaucracy, unstructured and ineffective governance, favouritism, unethical behaviours, imbalance performance reward etc.

- *Emergency situations* – include fire and flood. These are usually rare occurrences, and their impacts could be very transient.

- *Lack of adequate equipment*, tools and technologies, required to support the project, could cause frustration leading to stressful situations.

Stress can be managed and controlled. Stress management techniques and tips are widely published and you can reference them in your local library or on the Internet. Unmanaged stress leads to loss of productivity or poor quality outcome. It is important to manage stress in a responsible way, because it is better to be safe than sorry.

Networking

It is very valuable to know who to call and seek help from when you are in challenging or tough situations. Establishing personal and professional links could serve you well. The goal here is to emphasize the value of networking.

Your networks include the internal and external parties who could become great asset to you in your professional life. So seize opportunities to develop and build on them. It could be through personal and professional contact or online contact (for example, social networking like facebook.com, linkedin.com etc.). It does not cost you much; just pay some attention to it and it will pay off sometime. It is not usually one way, you may have something to offer to others, based on your experience, capability and skills, and others in your networks know it.

Identifying and seeking counsel from others, as a coach and/or a mentor, pays. Explore them in your workplace, professional gathering and other great avenues. Maintain good contact list of people in your networks. Keep networking at professional and social level, avoiding becoming part of a gossip network, political or rivalry camp within the organization.

Chapter 17 - Key Success Skills – Financial

"Sometimes one pays most for the things one gets for nothing."   *Albert Einstein*

No one wants to pay for things that do not provide a convincing and expected value. Every project must demonstrate its worth, else it could be considered of little or no value. A project manager needs a reasonable understanding of the project financial responsibility to demonstrate to the key stakeholders, particularly the sponsor, that the project is on track to deliver the desired outcome at the agreed and expected cost, time and quality. Treat it as a typical seller-buyer relationship. Essentially, you need solid understanding of project estimation and budgeting, financial performance tracking/monitoring and reporting.

Project Estimation and Budget

Project estimate is usually prepared by the project portfolio management group, prior to formal project approval and initiation, as part of the project conceptualization and business case development. A project manager needs good understanding of project cost estimation to ensure that cost accuracy, within tolerable limits, is maintained during the project life cycle, due to changes in scope and other factors such as inflation, technology etc. Organizations establish tolerable limits using the cost contingency range (measured in percentage) at different stages of the project life cycle.

The preferred or recommended approach to building the project cost estimate, which the client can relate to, is the result based costing. Result based costing is based on the project deliverables. This approach enables the client and stakeholders to trace the cost of delivering the desired project outcome.

Building the Cost Estimate

A professional will ensure that all costs are captured and avoid any attempt to hide cost in order to secure acceptable funding. Underestimation is a recipe for disaster, a major reason for project failure or mediocre outcome. Overestimation is neither a good thing, avoid it.

Underestimation and overestimation usually occur due to incompetency, organization attitudes or undue influence to control cost in a generic way. For example, the use of across the board cost cutting, which usually impact those who have done due diligence to present realistic cost. People tend to overestimate to catch up with the across the board cost cutting tactics. It is prudent to provide honest and valid estimate you can stand by and defend. Clients disrespect all attempts to overestimate or provide cost without clear justification.

Experienced, knowledgeable and ethical professionals know the importance of sound estimate that can be defended. For cost estimation you may use the top-down approach for a start and validate with a bottom-up approach. Otherwise, you should build the project cost using the bottom-up approach, which enables you to minimize cost contingency or changes in the future.

The key considerations for successful cost estimation include the following:

- Requirements - the key determinant of what the project will likely cost.

- Stakeholders/human capital - chargeable fees, resource types and rates.

- Materials/Equipment - capital and operating assets, facilities and tools.

- Administration - the overhead cost for managing the project and delivering the product.

Figure 17 shows a result based project cost estimation guide. The approach maps all cost to deliverables, which are combined to deliver the desired project outcome.

Notes on Over/Under Estimation

- Overestimation and underestimation should be avoided. Underestimation is rare, overestimation is common. The consequences of both are not desirable.

- Underestimation usually results in the delivery of poor or low quality product.

- Overestimation could be considered fraudulent. Sometimes it could be just to cover unexpected issues and risks. However, avoid situation where it could lead to project abandonment.

- Underestimation to reduce time and cost may end up costing you more money and time. Do not try to be '*penny wise and pound foolish*'.

- Do not provide estimate based on unclear needs or scope. Ask questions; do due diligence and state assumptions clearly.

- Cost may change; base it on justifiable or defendable reasons.

You might be thinking this is not real and no big deal, but a seriously business minded organization frown at careless estimates and you may loose respect over time. Even organizations which do not take their estimates seriously will do when they are dealing with limited resources and contending priorities.

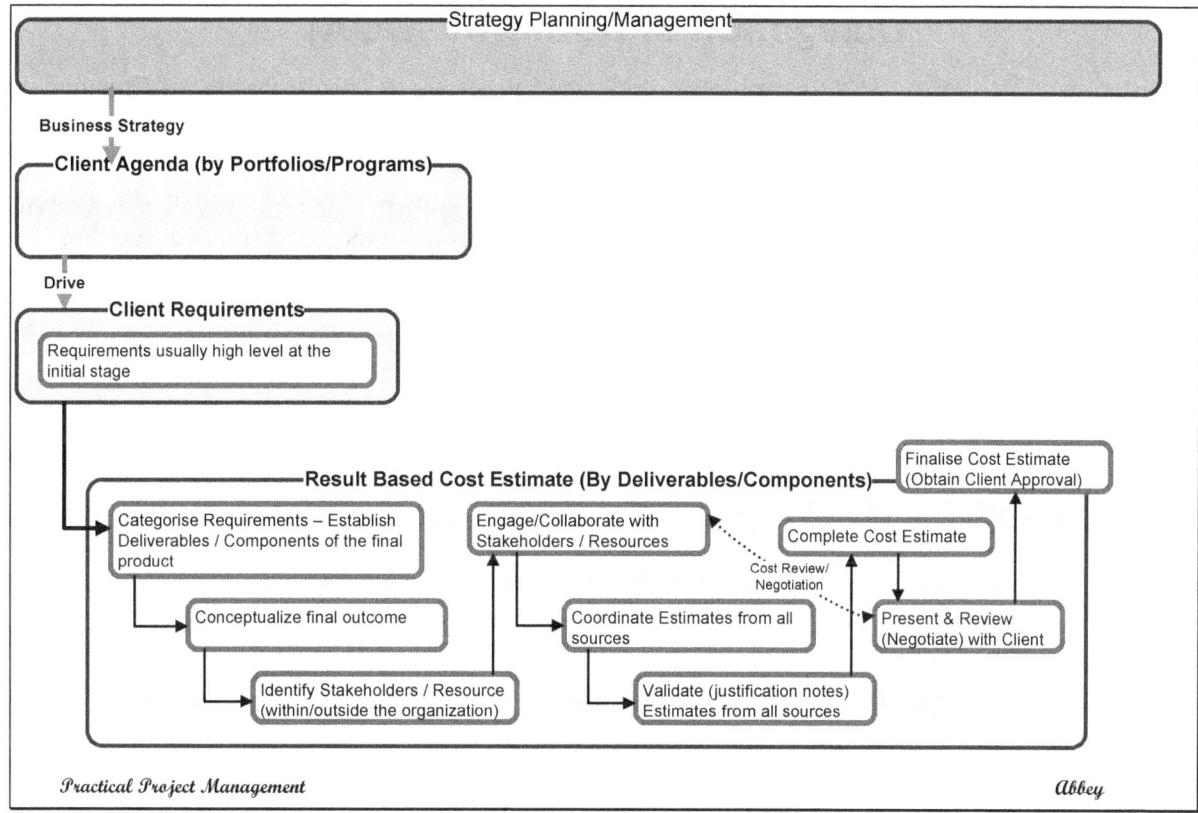

Figure 17 - Cost Estimation Guide

Table 7 includes a reference or link to a result based cost estimation workbook template.

Table 7 - Cost Estimate Template

PPMBook\ProjectManagement\PPM_CostEstimateTemplate.xls

Financial Performance Tracking and Reporting

"Not everything that counts can be counted and not everything that can be counted counts."
                                                                    Albert Einstein

A financial report should focus on what is relevant and useful for the stakeholders. Trying to report all possible financial records could overwhelm the audience and may dilute or hide vital information for decision making. The importance of relevant and valuable financial information cannot be understated. The content of a financial report, including the template, is discussed in Part 6 (Deliver Result).

Delegation of Authority (DOA)

Delegation of Authority (DOA) stipulates guidelines and rules to ensure quality of financial and related activities, by enforcing limited accountability at different assignment levels within the organization. This is a major requirement for auditing and responsible enforcement of financial dealings and service request approvals. It is not about whether or not you are trusted, it is about due diligence to ensure efficient and effective project cost performance tracking and prevent undue abuse of assigned roles and responsibilities.

As a project manager, you need to understand the DOA for your organization in order to effectively plan and secure approvals of key financial related activities for your project(s). You should accommodate the DOA reviews and approvals turn-around in the project plan (schedule). The DOA key elements are included in the Project Checklist section, Part 6 (Deliver Result).

Chapter 18 - Key Success Skills – Others

Ethics

Every profession has its own ethics or code of professional practice which guide the work behaviours. It cuts across organizational boundaries. Project Management Institute (PMI®) calls this Professional Responsibility.

Key ethics, among others, include:

- Be honest: there is difference between diplomacy and misrepresentation.

- Do not take bribe: expression of gratitude is not illegal, but does not have to be fulfilled.

- Gifts: know and follow your organization guidelines for gifts received from third parties and partners.

- Respect contract/agreements' terms and conditions.

- Negotiate in good faith. Otherwise a party who felt cheated may have a hidden resentment or vengeance attitude, which could materialise in future dealings.

Administration

As a project manager, sometimes you may find yourself juggling different administrative tasks, particularly if you do not have a dedicated project support analyst on your project, depending on your organization setup and specific project need. Administrative tasks include gathering information, preparing for meetings and managing minutes, monitoring and recording action items, work schedule, status reports and agreements.

The key to success is to minimize the number of reports or consolidate your reports into relevant categories, which address the unique need of the stakeholder groups. Keep vital information such as project profile as a single source and use it in applicable reports.

Some organizations have automated enterprise project management systems, which generate reports on the fly and manage projects' information (storage, distribution and work flow). The key challenge is the discipline to maintain quality data required by such information system in order to generate accurate reports.

Composure

A project manager needs to maintain his/her composure, particularly in tough situations and times. Being composed is a sign of maturity. It does not mean lack of concern. Though you may be troubled inside, loosing your composure in the presence of the team/stakeholders may weaken their performance and resilience to face tough situations. As an analogy (stated earlier): a project manager could be likened to a General in the army who faces a tough battle. Though he is troubled inside, he has to summon courage to act skilfully and inspiringly, without loosing his composure in order to motivate and strengthen the troops.

Maintaining your composure enhances your ability to make good decisions and operate effectively. To do this, you need to understand yourself and develop appropriate strategies to manage stress and stressful situations. Doing otherwise may cause more problem than you are trying to solve. You may be the last hope to straighten crooked situations in your project. Hence maintaining your composure is a great virtue.

Tools

Skilful and effective use of tools will help you manage work, communicate expectations and report outcome. Use tools to convey the right message to the target audience. The most important thing is the clarity of the content of the document, not necessarily how fanciful the document is. A project manager should be versatile in using some tools like those listed bellow:

- Project management: Scheduling (Microsoft Project, Clarity, Workbench); Planning, brainstorming, problem solving and decision making (Mindjet Mind Manager Pro or similar mind mapping tool).

- Office productivity: Document, charts, analysis and presentation (Microsoft® Word, Excel, PowerPoint and Visio or Open Source equivalent - e.g. Sun® OpenOffice).

- Financial systems: Estimating, forecasting, budgeting, account payable etc.

There are many good tools, including those that support full automation. However, without practical project management practices, including stakeholders' discipline in providing relevant and quality information, you may not be able to explore or take advantage of the automation capabilities of these tools. Tools provide control information, but exercising control requires sound governance, skills, discipline and good judgement.

Part 5 – Product Delivery Management

This part includes the following topics:

- Product Life Cycle

- Product Delivery Management - Generic

- Product Delivery Management - Industry Specific

Blank page

Chapter 19 - Product Life Cycle

The importance of product management is evident within the context of the product life cycle. In a broader sense, product management covers product delivery, product support and product retirement.

Figure 18 shows the product life cycle stages and the application of product management within these stages. Product life cycle is a complete life span of a product covering introduction, growth, maturity, decline, extension (where possible) and retirement. Product management provides the processes and practices for managing product within (or at each stage of) the product life cycle.

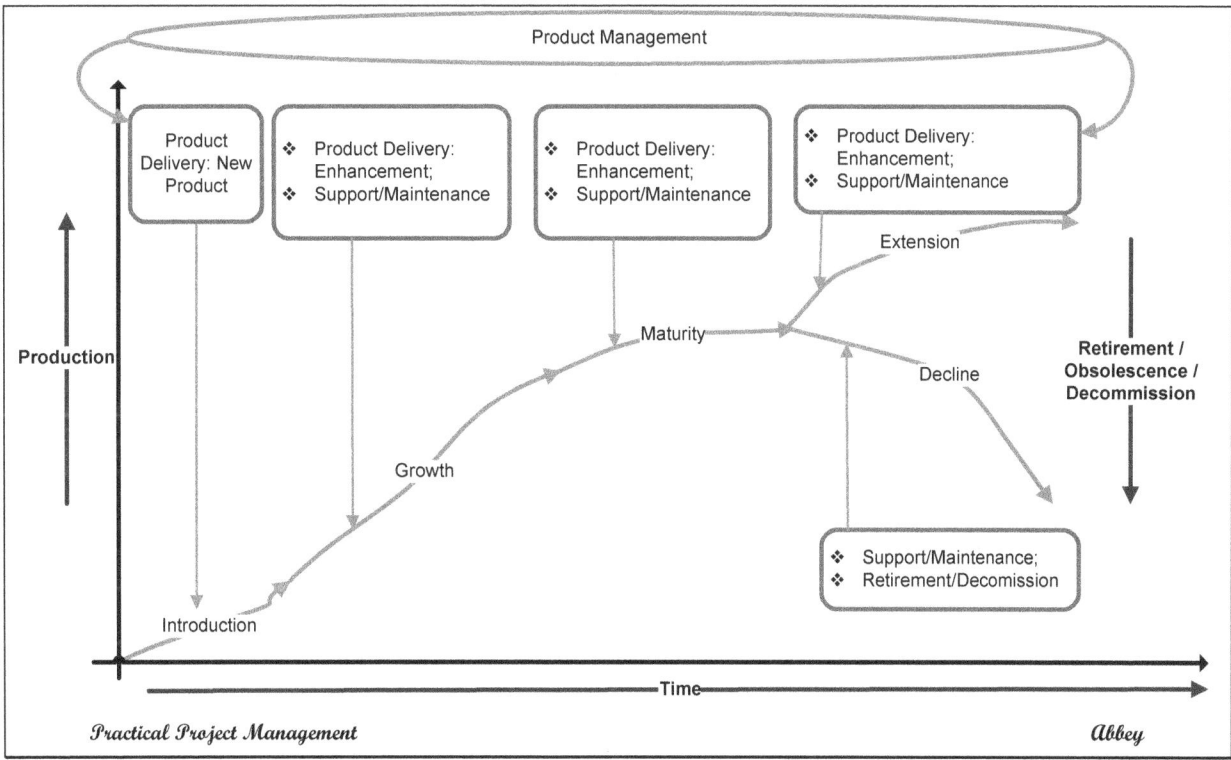

Figure 18 - Product Life Cycle

Product Delivery Management - Generic

Project delivery management emphasizes an aspect of product management within the project life cycle. A generic product delivery management framework is shown in Figure 19. The typical processes include project idea or concept, product requirements, product design, product construction, testing and sign-off, and commissioning (transition to operations or product support).

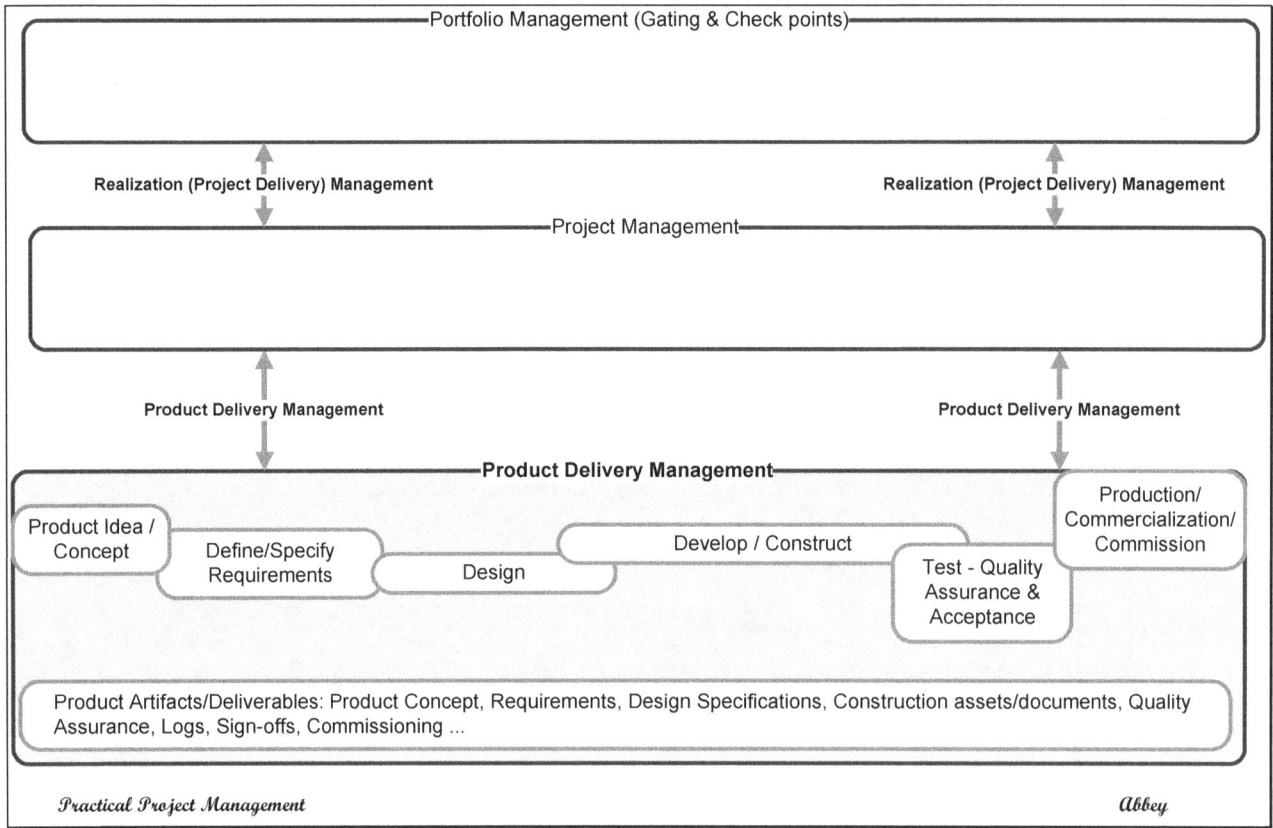

Figure 19 - Product Delivery Management, Generic framework

Ideally pre-production/commissioning sign-off follows the user acceptance testing. As part of the project close-out, client's closing sign-off occurs after the commissioning or production release. The post production issues are addressed during the post production support phase and as specified in the SLA.

Chapter 20 - Product Delivery Management - Industry Specific

Project management cuts across different industries, while product delivery management is industry specific. The matured industry specific product delivery management processes, including their interactions with the project management processes, will be briefly described.

Product delivery management processes and practices fulfill the delivery of new, enhanced or modified products within the product life cycle. It begins at the conceptualization phase, progressing to design, development, production and commercialization. The vital role of project management is to ensure that well thought through processes and practices are applied to ensure that the right product is delivered, using the appropriate product delivery management processes and practices.

Some organizations have integrated or harmonized the project management and product delivery management processes into a unified framework. However, this does not preclude the separate significance of the two related but interdependent disciplines.

Sometimes, the product delivery organization may be an external service provider. Therefore, it is advisable to have a contract document or agreement, signed by the project manager and the product delivery manager, defining the product specifications and governing the expectations.

Information Management and Technology

The methodologies described here are used to develop custom built solutions and implement Commercial Off-The-shelve Solutions (COTS). To understand the delivery of Information Technology (IT) based solutions (application, data/information, security and infrastructure), it is important to briefly describe some de-facto industry frameworks or methodologies that are commonly used and adapted to deliver these solutions.

In most organizations, particularly in small to medium size organizations, the complete understanding of these frameworks is rare. This is because some part of the organization focuses on the application of one or some of the frameworks, without a good appreciation of the complements that others provide. Understanding these frameworks, including their applications and how they complement each other, is very important to establish and sustain service excellence.

COBIT - Governance/Management

Control OBjectives for Information and related Technology (COBIT) is an IT governance, service planning, delivery, control and support framework. COBIT is a set of best practices and framework for information technology (IT) management created by the Information Systems Audit and Control Association (ISACA), and the IT Governance Institute (ITGI) in 1992. COBIT provides managers, auditors, professionals and information technology users with a set of generally accepted measures, indicators, processes and best practices to assist them in maximizing the benefits derived through the use of information technology and developing appropriate IT governance and control in the organization. Detailed information on COBIT is available at the isaca.org website.

Figure 20 shows a representation of the COBIT 4.1 framework. COBIT 4.1 has 34 high level processes that cover 210 control objectives categorized in four domains - Plan and Organize, Acquire and Implement, Deliver and Support, and Monitor and Evaluate. COBIT provides benefits to managers, IT users, professionals and auditors. Managers benefit from COBIT because it provides them with a foundation upon which IT related decisions and investments can be based on. It provides the IT professionals with the framework to deliver products and services that maximize value for the users of IT products and services.

COBIT provides end-to-end picture of IT products and services delivery and management. Its understanding will enable a project manager to appreciate the relevance of project delivery within the overall context of IT service delivery.

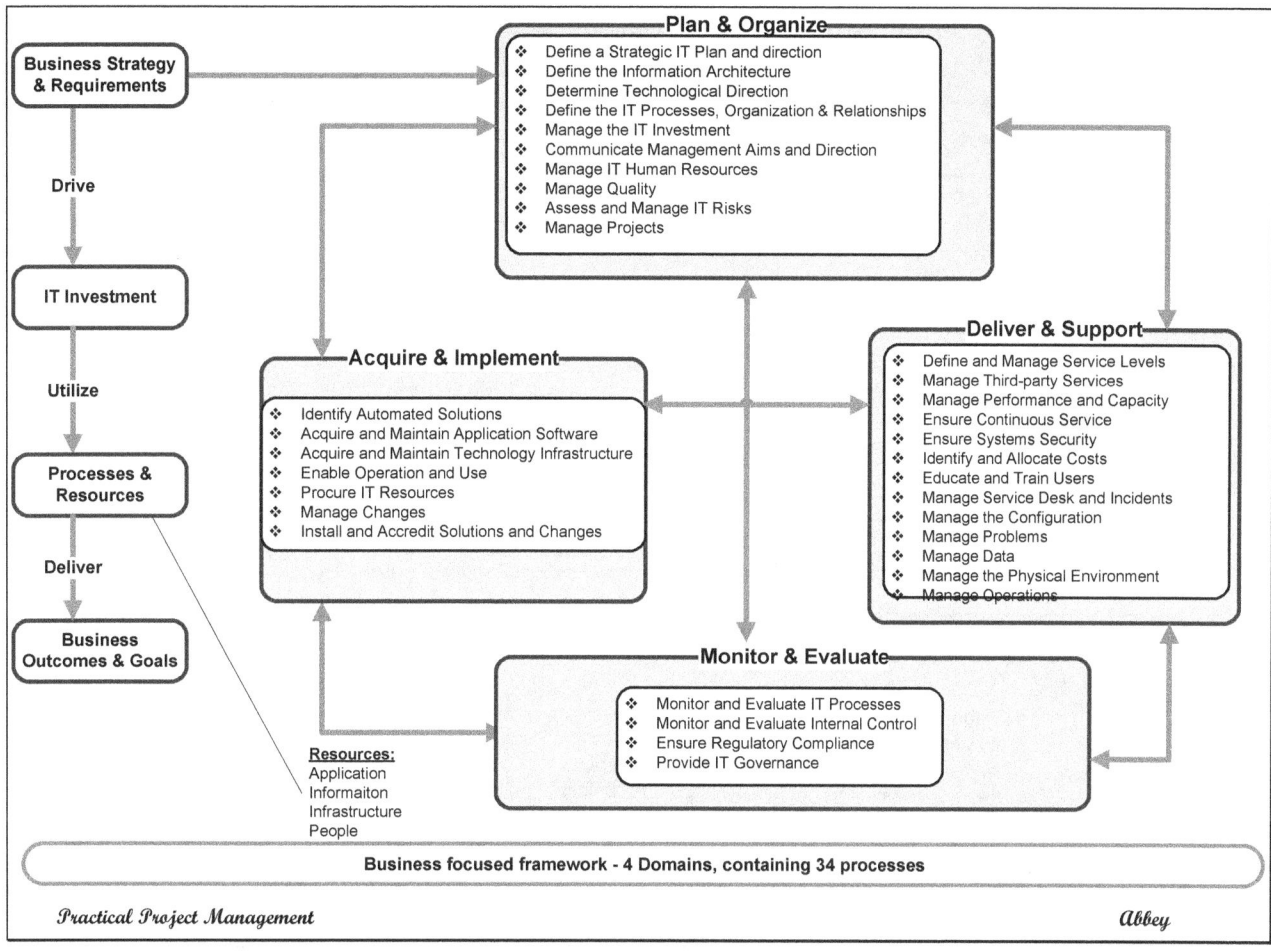

Figure 20 - COBIT Framework – An Overview Representation

Information Systems Delivery Methodology - SDLC

System Development Life Cycle (SDLC) is a tested and widely used IT based business solutions development methodology. It provides the framework for structuring, planning, designing, developing and delivering information systems. The traditional SDLC phases are feasibility study, requirement analysis, design, development (construction), testing, implementation and post implementation review.

Variations of the traditional SDLC exist, with customized characteristics. However, the goal of each variation or type is the same - to deliver information technology solutions that meet the defined and agreed client requirements or needs in a timely and cost effective fashion. Figure 21 is a representation of the SDLC framework. It shows the processes and their associated deliverables.

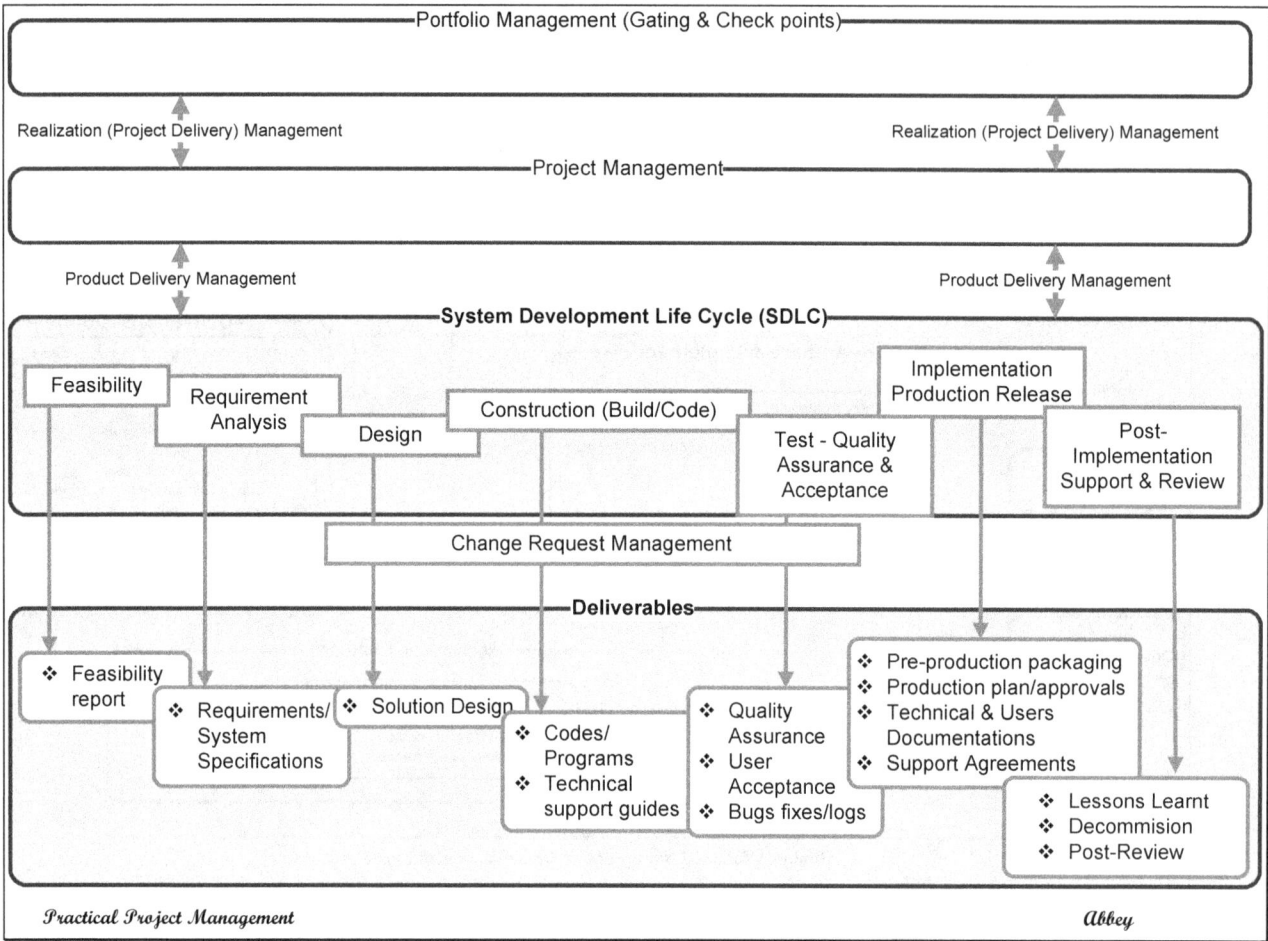

Figure 21 - System Development Life Cycle (SDLC)

Information Systems Delivery Methodology – RUP

Rational Unified Process (RUP) is an IBM® version of the SDLC. It has been proven to be reliable for conceptualizing, analyzing, designing, developing and deploying IT based business solutions. It supports different approaches (waterfall, iterative or mixed) to solutions delivery. Figure 22 is a representation of the RUP methodology. It shows the processes and their associated deliverables.

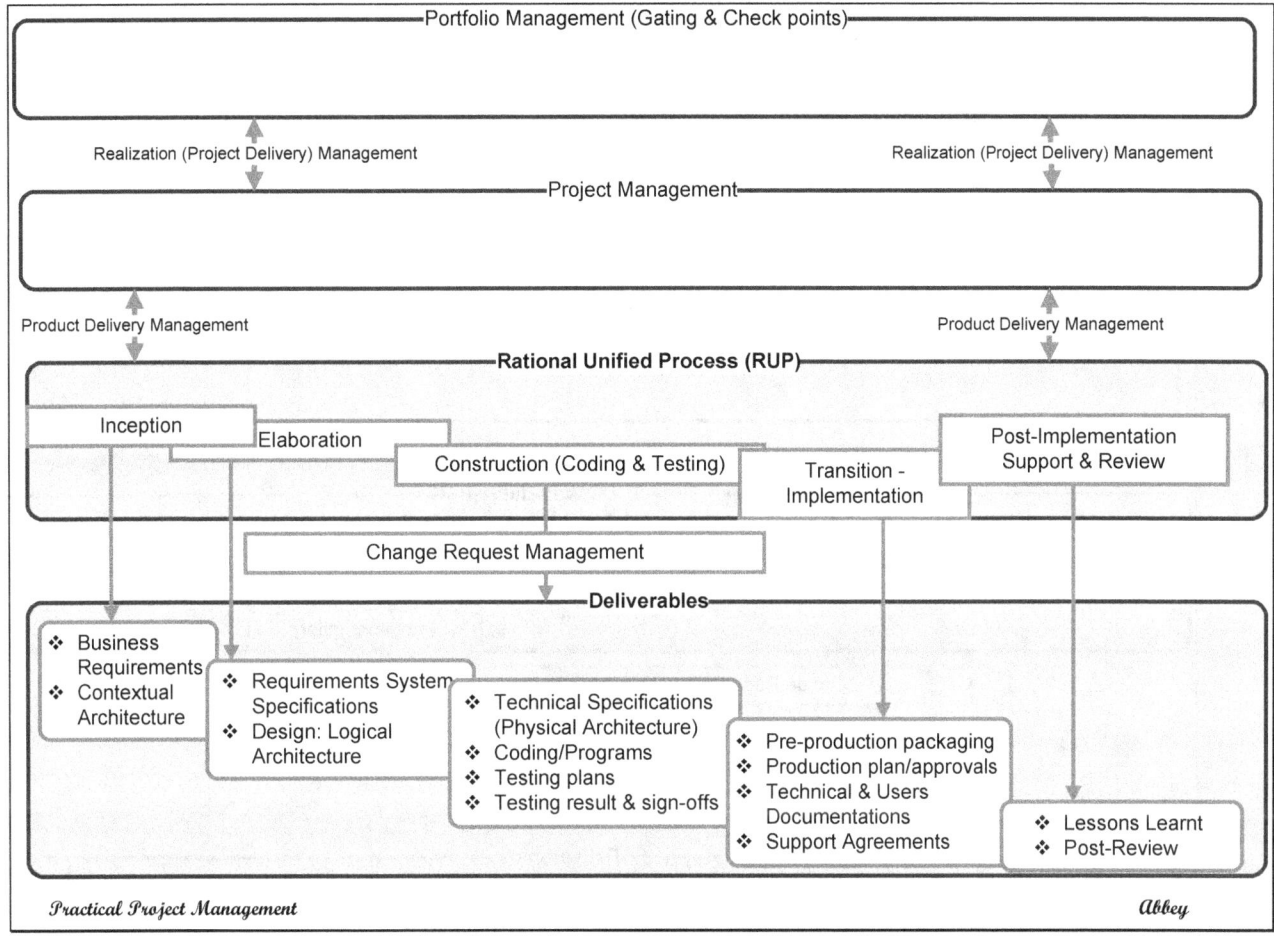

Figure 22 - Rational Unified Process (RUP)

Information Systems Delivery Methodology – Approach

There are two basic approaches to developing and delivering IT based business solutions - waterfall and iterative. Variations of these two, particularly iterative, exist. The focus here is on these two basic approaches.

Waterfall: This a sequential, though with some overlaps, approach to transform user requirements into system specifications, design, development and delivery of a solution that meets the user requirements. It is generally adopted in matured environments where user requirements are known to a high degree, with high confidence and minimal or no change in the course of solution or product development.

Iterative: This is a progressive incremental approach to developing information systems. It is commonly used for new product development, where requirements are not well established and need to emerge over time. The SDLC method is applied in phases to elicit stage by stage, analysis, design and development of known requirements into a solution. It goes through series of progressive iterations where additional requirements are identified, sometimes through proto-types.

The SDLC (or RUP) methodology does not prescribe a specific approach. The SDLC is used, albeit in different fashion, in both waterfall and iterative approaches. Figure 23 and Figure 24 show the use of the SDLC methodology in the waterfall and iterative approaches respectively.

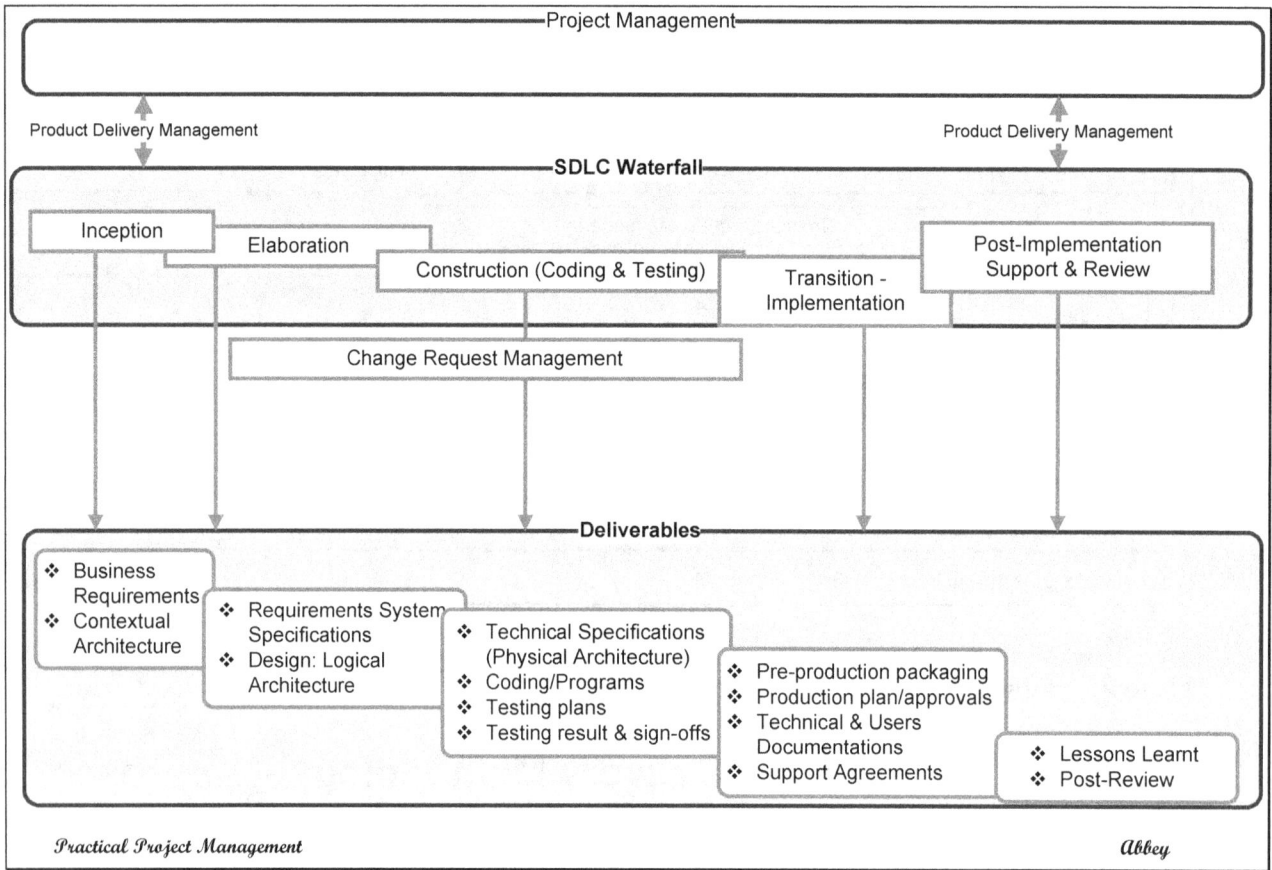

Figure 23 - Product Delivery Management, SDLC Waterfall

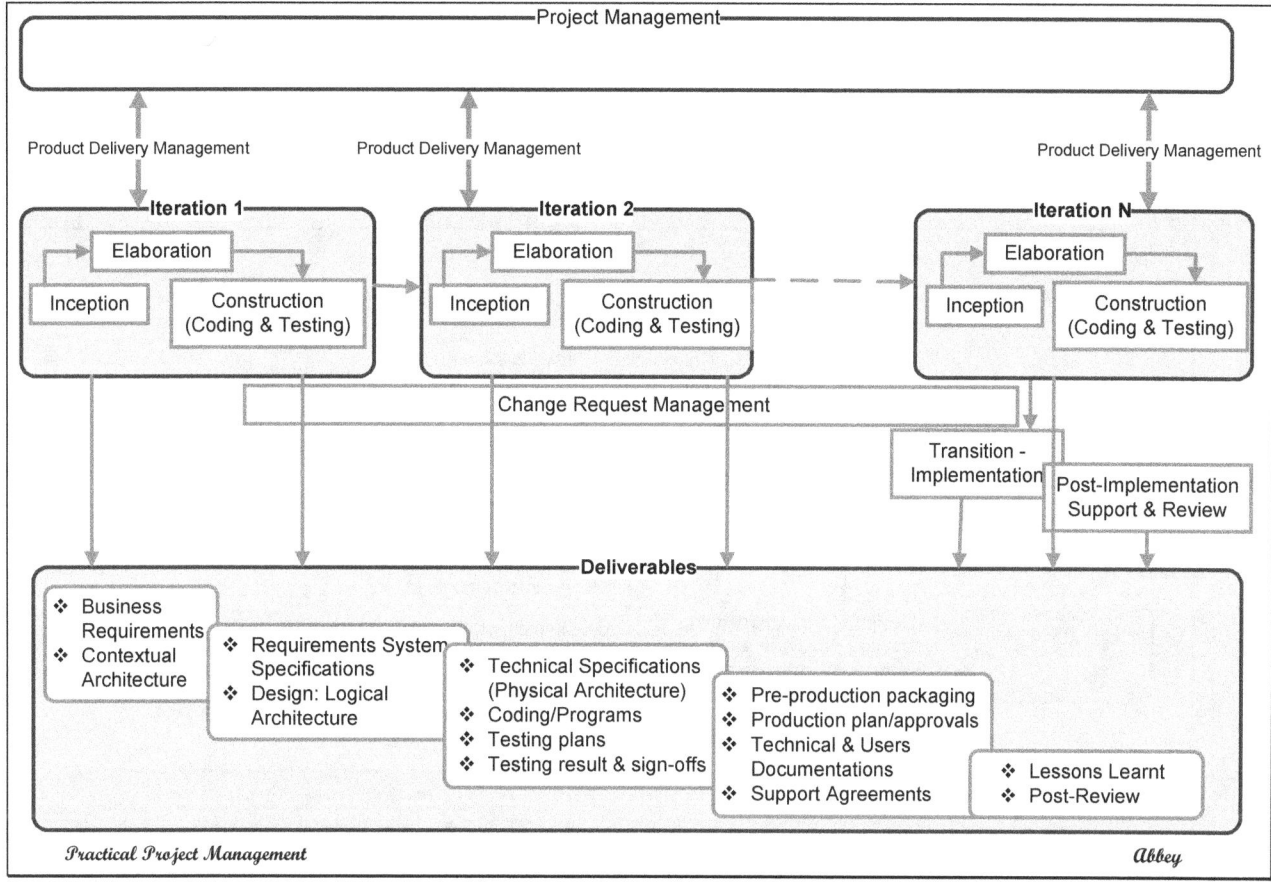

Figure 24 - Product Delivery Management, SDLC Iterative

Infrastructure Delivery Methodology

Infrastructure includes hardware and software (operating system, middle ware, support and utility software). It is the platform on which the business solutions (application and data) run. It requires specific or customized fit-for-purpose methodology to ensure consistent delivery and sustenance.

ITIL (Information Technology Infrastructure Library, currently at version 3) is a de-facto service delivery and management framework which can be used or customized to deliver and manage infrastructure products and services. Also, the RUP methodology can be adapted to deliver infrastructure projects.

Basically, infrastructure product or service delivery follow these processes - inception (requirements specification), design/capacity planning, acquisition of equipment, software and service support, implementation and transition to operations.

Figure 25 shows an infrastructure delivery framework.

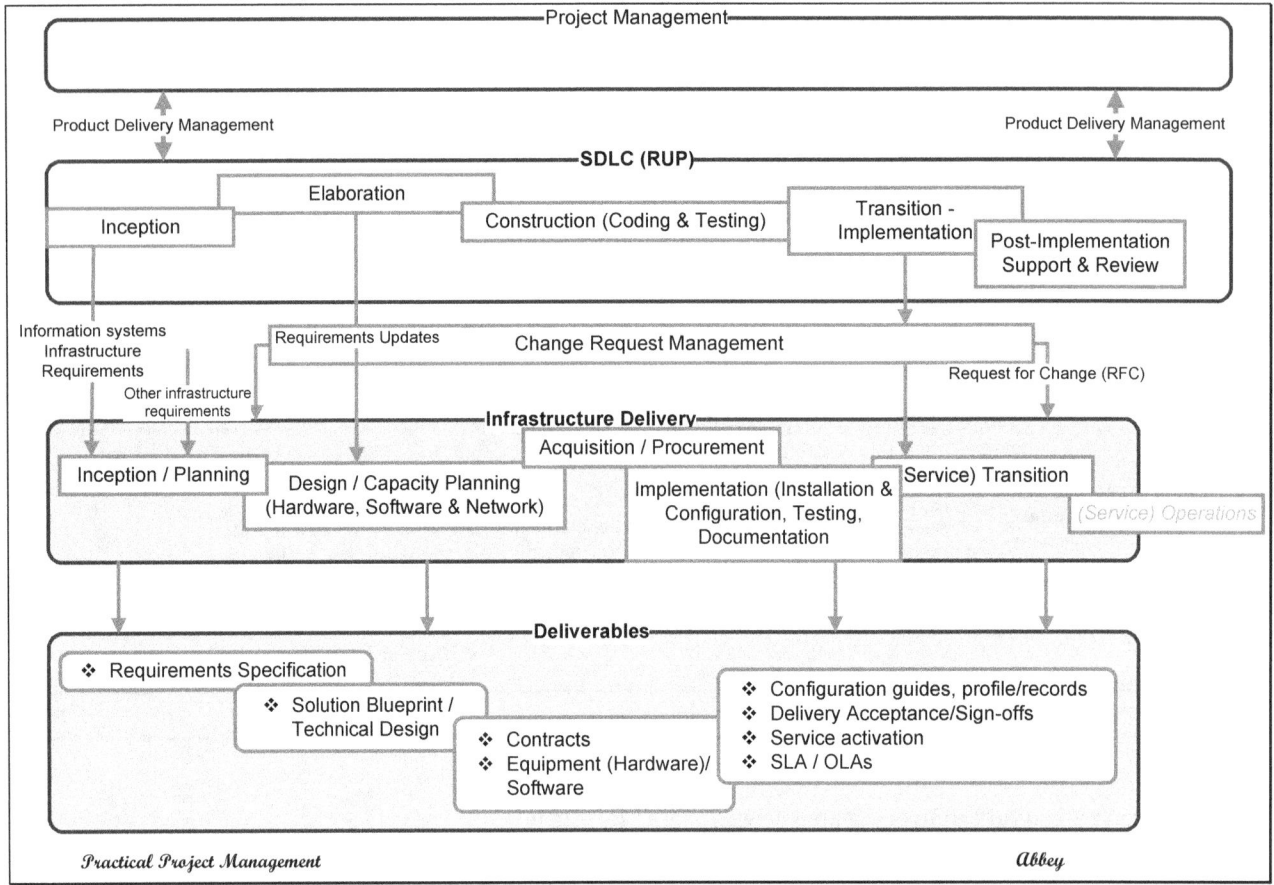

Figure 25 - Infrastructure Delivery

Notes:

SLA ➜ Service Level Agreement is the service support or sustainment (contractual) agreement between an organization and the (third party) service delivery partner or organization.

OLA ➜ Operational Level Agreement is the service support or sustainment (contractual) agreement between the service delivery teams within the same organization. For example, an OLA may exist between the application development/maintenance and technology/hosting service delivery teams.

Information Systems Delivery Methodology - COTS

Commercial Off The Shelve (COTS) products are third party solutions that can be purchased, configured and/or customized to meet the client needs. Examples of COTs include SAP (System Application Program) - an enterprise resource planning and industry solutions portfolio, Oracle® Financials and PeopleSoft HR. Figure 26 shows a COTS delivery framework.

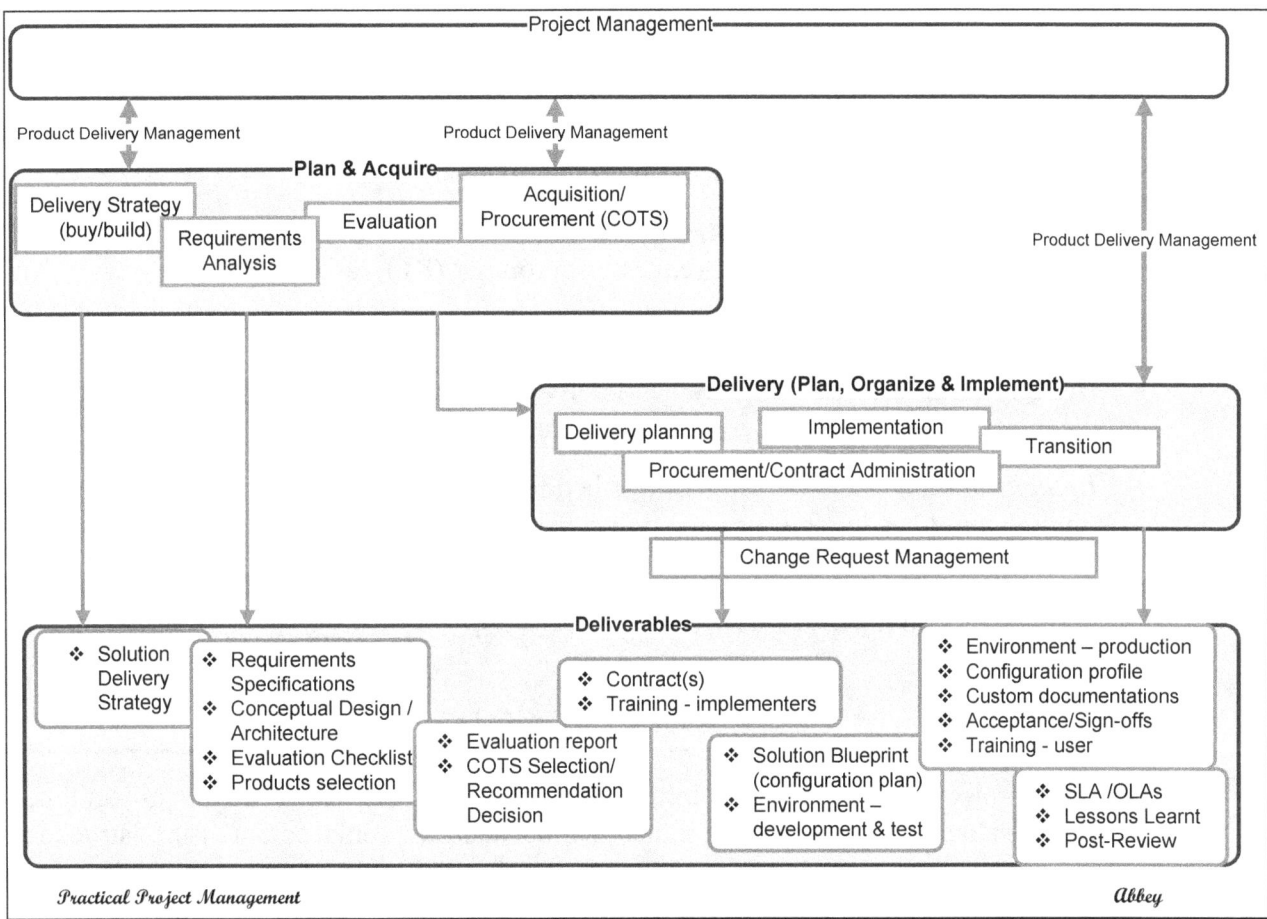

Figure 26 - COTS Delivery

COTS delivery framework can be categorized into two parts: (i) Plan & Acquire and (ii) Delivery (Plan, Organize & Implement).

Plan & Acquire includes the following key elements:

- ▪ **Product delivery strategy**: a decision has to be made by the organization to build or buy a new product, based on the organization's strategy or a specific need.

- **Requirements specification**: for COTS solution, the requirements have to be defined and specified in great detail to ensure that the right or best-fit product is selected for implementation.

- **Evaluation checklist**: this is derived from the requirements specification. It presents the requirements in format that facilitate features comparison across the selected third party products.

- **Product Selection**: products are selected for evaluation based on preliminary reviews (e.g. request for information and vendors' demonstration) of possible products.

- **Evaluation**: evaluation of selected products is performed using the evaluation checklist. A product, with the lowest trade-off, is usually selected based on the evaluation result and recommendation.

- **COTS decision and acquisition**: this is a procurement process to acquire the selected product(s), usually through the request for proposal (RFP) activities.

Delivery (Plan, Organize & Implement) includes the following key elements:

- **Delivery Plan**: the main deliverable of delivery planning is the solution blueprint for the infrastructure setup and software configuration.

- **Implementation**: includes setup of test-bed for customization and/or configuration, training, pilot, testing, pre-production packaging, acceptance and production release.

- **Transition**: includes creation of support agreements, commission, decommission and post-production release review.

Construction

Construction projects vary in type, discipline, complexity and size. Construction project types include new product or asset, existing product maintenance and replacement or infrastructure renewals. Some maintenance work, depending on the size and organization, may not be treated as project, but rather as a minor work order, which usually takes less than 30 days to complete. An example of a minor work order is the repairs of a minor fracture on a portion of a local road.

Construction projects usually involve professionals from various disciplines (mechanical, electrical, civil and chemical engineering, finance, information technology etc.) working together at various stages of the project.

Examples of construction projects include:

- Transportation - road construction, maintenance or renewal.

- Housing/Building - home, office, school construction, maintenance or renewal.

- Factory/industrial construction.

- Chemicals - flow station, refinery construction, maintenance or renewal.

- Electrical - new power station, sub-station and new transmission lines.

- Mechanical - new automobile production or re-branding, new aircraft for department of defense.

Essentially key processes for a typical construction project include:

- Requirements - Requirement Specifications.

- Planning & Conceptual Design.

- Procurement / Contract Administration.

- Detailed Design.

- Construction & Delivery (Acceptance).

- Commission/Decommission.

Figure 27 shows a construction product delivery management framework.

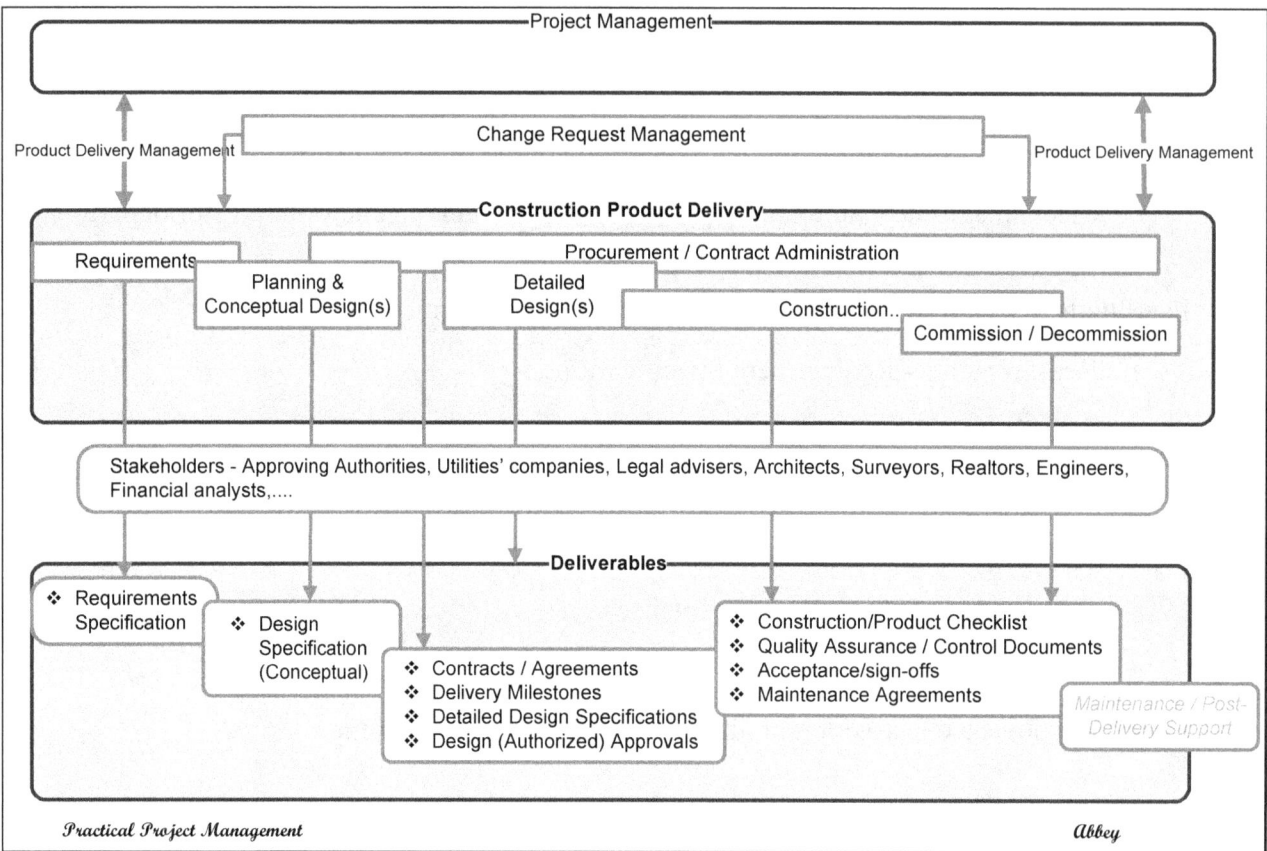

Figure 27 - Construction Product Delivery Management

Part 6: Managing Outcome - Deliver Result

This part includes the following topics:

- Project Setup and Planning

- Integrated Project Management Plan

- Deliverables Checklist

- Monitoring and Controlling

- Communication

- Supporting Activities

- Implementation

- Closing

- Good Practices

Blank page

Chapter 21 - Deliver Result

"I never worry about action, but only inaction."   *Winston Churchill*

Your performance is maximized on projects that you believe in and are passionate about. You can only be at your best or on top of your game, if you are passionate about or enjoy what you are doing. Now, the project is approved for implementation, what is next?

The focus here is on taking actions to ensure that the project goals are realized. This is the stage where the rubber meets the road. This is the reality check, when you plan and execute the agenda. Things that count at this stage are deliverables, deliverables and deliverables. This is where you apply your knowledge, skills, experiences, good judgment, methodologies, techniques, tools and good practices. *Every action should be clearly defined, developed, measured, controlled and improved upon to accomplish the desired result*.

The combination of processes, techniques, tools and, very importantly, good practices are critical to the successful delivery of the desired project outcome. What you do at this stage will determine the outcome, which will be tested as the rubber meets the road at each major step towards fulfilling the project mandate and goals.

In order to successfully deliver the desired project outcome, you need to balance your relationship with the project stakeholders and result-orientation. Figure 28 shows the relationship-result matrix and key characteristics exhibited at each level. The directions of the arrows show the preferred and desired target state, where the project team should be in order to operate at the optimal level.

Effective communication is crucial to successful project delivery. Silence does not necessarily mean consent. If in doubt, ask and ensure you obtain a response. Behaviours to watch for and carefully manage to ensure success and prevent avoidable problems include:

- Passive aggressive behaviours.

- No sense of urgency to get things done. This may lead to slackness and endless delays.

- Operation mode behaviours, particularly responses that are generally reactive and not carefully thought out or based on trial and error. This usually leads to taking action without thinking through the implications.

- Domineering type of behaviours. That is, my way or no way. Move the team towards having healthy debates, not suppressing any ideas without providing persuasive and better alternatives.

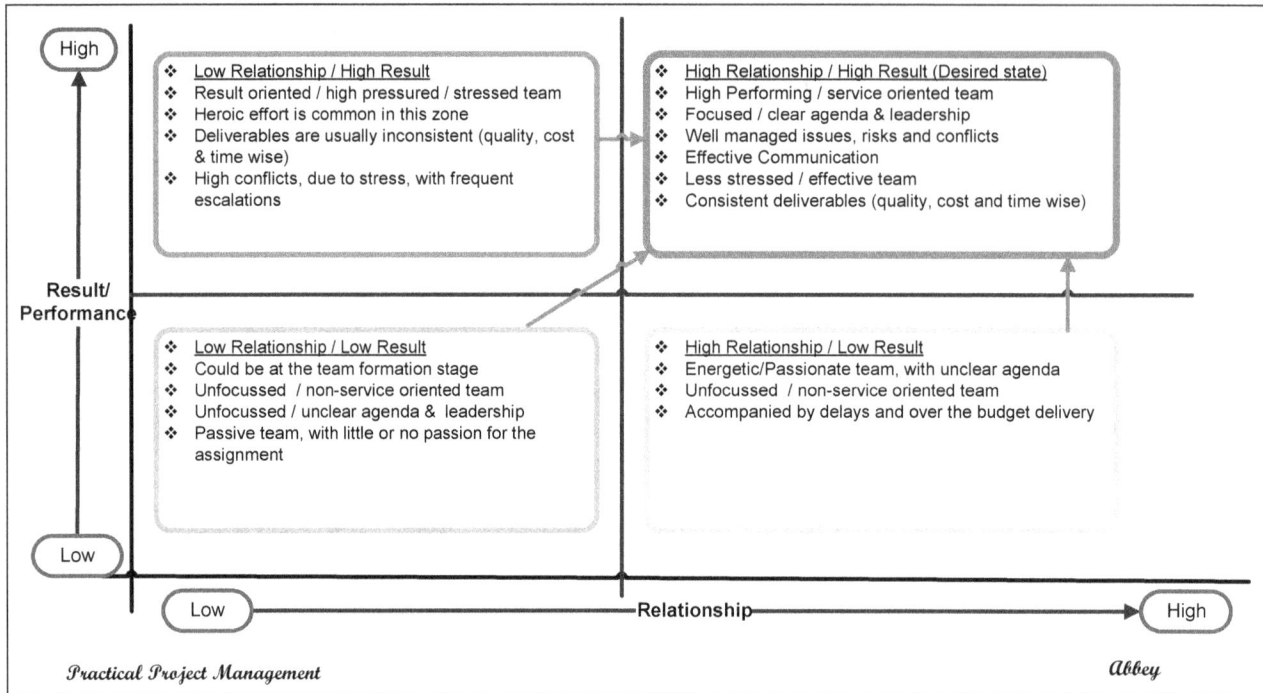

Figure 28 - Relationship & Result/Performance Matrix

Next, each component of the Managing Outcome - Deliver Result, will be examined. We will carefully and thoughtfully examine the key steps in project delivery planning and managing the plan towards a successful project outcome. It is important to be passionate; however, unrealistic, narrow view and uncontrolled or unmanaged behaviours and practices lead to unnecessary conflicts and sometimes frustration. For instance, trying to solve problem, without proper analysis may lead to no solution, or at best mediocre solution.

Figure 29 shows the approach to managing the project and delivering result, successfully. ***This approach demonstrates how the <u>people</u> utilize proven <u>processes</u> and <u>tools</u> to deliver <u>results.</u>***

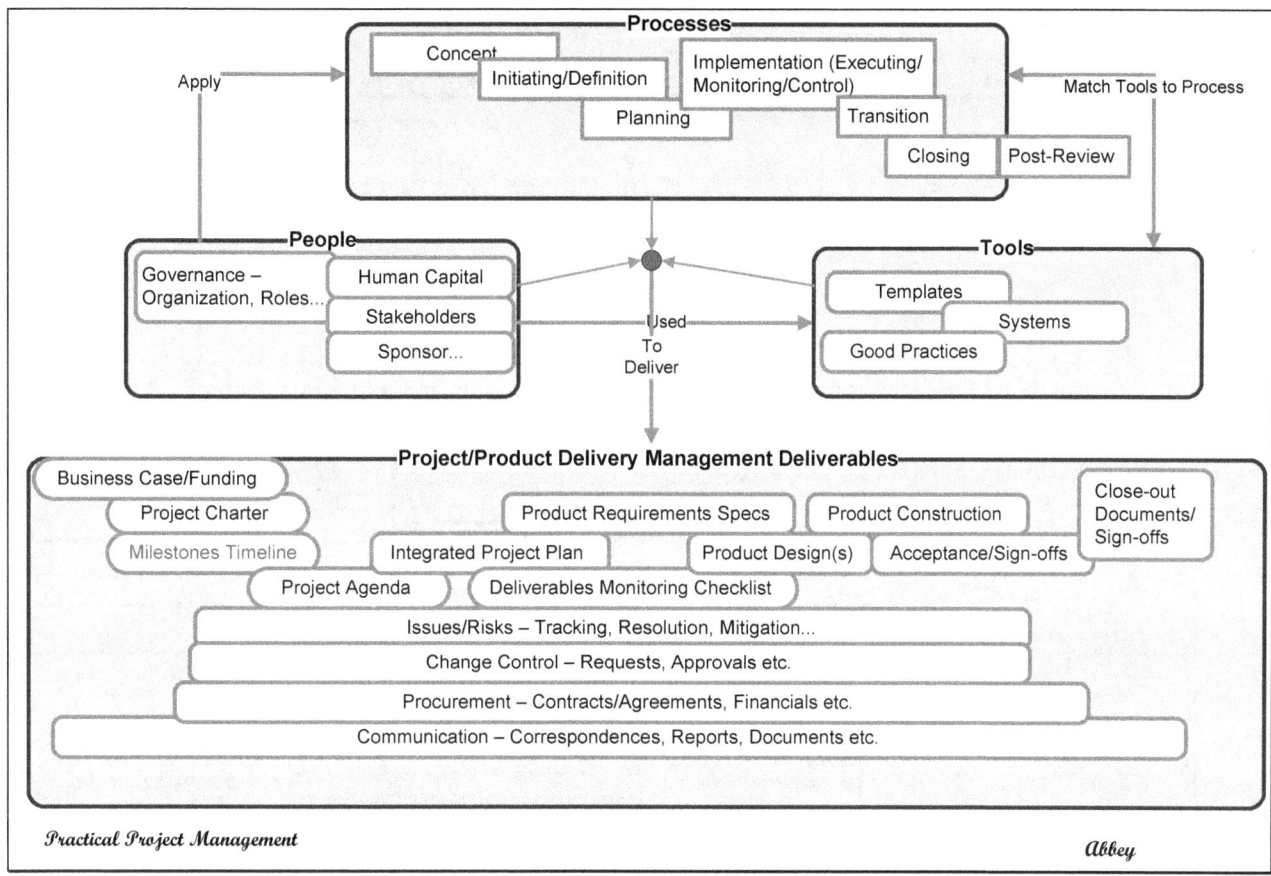

Figure 29 - PPM Deliver Result, Approach

Figure 30 shows the comprehensive overview of a practical project delivery framework.

Figure 30 will be used as the reference to discuss the rest of Part 6. Sample templates are included where applicable. Templates provided may be modified to suit your needs, in case you do not have existing and approved templates.

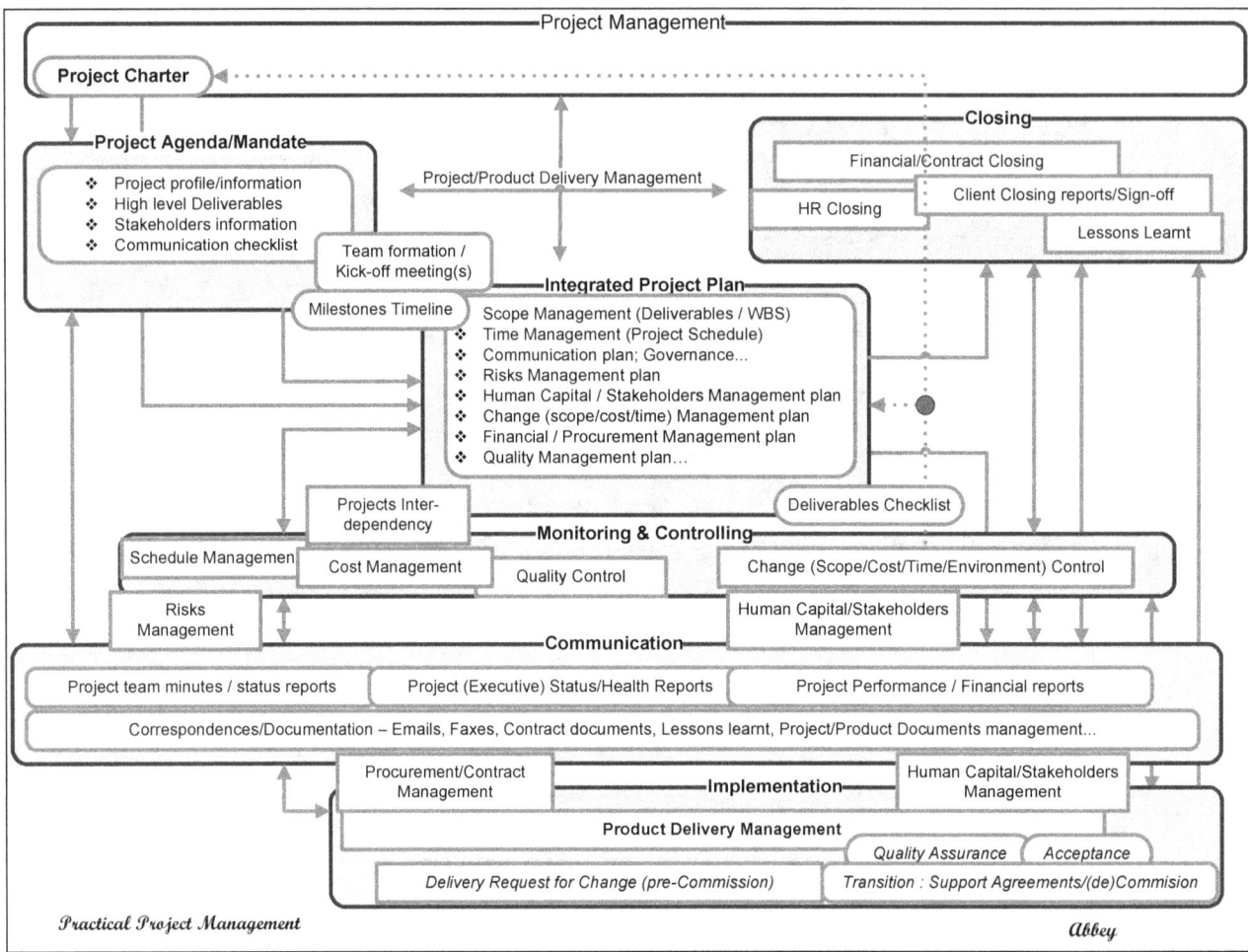

Figure 30 - Deliver Result - Key Steps

To successfully deliver your project, ensure that the project team members are competent and matured professionals, with the right and positive attitudes, including team work and leadership qualities. Otherwise, you may be in a struggling state throughout the life cycle of the project. Solid and responsible human capital is the backbone of your projects' success stories.

Chapter 22 - Project Setup and Planning

The focus here is to seek understanding of the project mission, goals and desired outcome. Effective project kick-off is a key success factor to delivering a project successfully. The goal of the kick-off meeting is to share, discuss and understand the project vision, mandate and expectations of the project. Project kick-off involves engagement of the stakeholders, particularly the core project team members, resources, techniques and tools to facilitate the successful planning, management and delivery of the project.

The key here is to do the first thing first. Following the successful completion of the project kick-off meeting is the project planning session. The goal of the project planning session(s) is (are) to review the scope of work, create the implementation roadmap, including the key steps to accomplish the desired outcome.

Project Charter

Ideally, project charter should be created, as a mandate or terms of reference document, for the project manager to implement the project. In reality, the project manager may have to create, update or coordinate the creation of the project charter. A project charter usually includes the following elements, not in any particular order:

- Project profile: includes project name, owner, projected start and end dates, and key stakeholders.

- Executive summary: includes project strategic goal, desired outcome, business drivers, summary of deliverables, timeline, cost and benefits.

- Project background: includes historical perspective, needs met or problem that will be solved.

- Scope: 'in' and 'out of' scope.

- High level milestones timeline.

- Cost, benefits and funding (budget).

- Project management approach: it defines the use of applicable methodology and techniques to plan and manage the project.

- High level risk assessment and impact analysis: includes qualitative impact analysis and risk mitigations.

- Assumptions and constraints.

- Project critical success factors.

- Performance measures: it defines the criteria for measuring the project outcome success, for client acceptance.

- Stakeholders, their interests, expectations and communication needs.

- Governance: includes project organization, stakeholders' roles and responsibilities.

- Change management guideline: describes how changes will be managed, that is, assessed and approved by the authorized stakeholders.

- Approvals by authorized stakeholders.

The content of the project charter is project dependent. For instance, the elements above may contain varying degree of details. In some cases, small projects may combine project charter and integrated project plan. Project charter ensures that you have a clearly defined mandate or terms of reference to authorize the implementation of an approved project. At the minimum, the project charter should contain the project goal and scope, cost and funding, risk management, deliverables timeline, stakeholders' interests and measurable expectations, and approvals. Table 8 includes a reference or link to the project charter template.

Table 8 - Project Charter Template

PPMBook\DeliverResult\PPM_ProjectCharter.doc

Project Agenda/Mandate

The project agenda is the first working document (optional, but recommended) you should create when you are assigned to play the role of a project manager or lead a project. You may call it a name that makes sense to you, the key here is the purpose and content of the document. It enables the project manager to have a good understanding of the project goals, scope, deliverables, cost and time constraints, and stakeholders' expectations. This working document will be useful in creating or updating other key project documents, such as project charter and integrated project plan, and managing the project. It is particularly useful in a situation where the project charter has not been created.

The components of the project agenda document include:

- Project profile: includes project name, enterprise unique number or ID, goal, description, approved project budget, time constraint, project manager, sponsor, champion and client's organization.

- High level deliverables: list of deliverables required to deliver the desired outcome.

- Stakeholders' information: includes stakeholders' contact information and stakeholder-influence matrix (discussed in Part 4 - Project Management, see page 74).

- Communication checklist: includes stakeholder group information needs, format and frequency.

Table 9 includes a reference or link to the project agenda template.

Table 9 - Project Agenda Template

PPMBook\DeliverResult\PPM_ProjectAgenda.doc

Depending on the project, some of the contents of the project agenda document could be extracted from the project charter (if it exists) and rolled over to the integrated project plan document.

Milestones Timeline

Having a clear implementation roadmap is critical to the successful delivery of a project. The deliverables that are required to develop a product or service are vital to developing high level single point accountability and responsibility. The roadmap can be represented in form of a timeline. The timeline is usually created at the preliminary phase prior to developing a full blown work breakdown structure (WBS) and project schedule.

The milestones timeline is very useful for discussing milestones progress with the stakeholders, particularly the executives and sponsor. It is a practical tool for engaging project team members during the kick-off meeting, planning discussions and ongoing milestones tracking, communication, monitoring and control. It is a live document which should be kept up-to-date and in sync with the project schedule milestones, based on the approved changes during the project delivery life cycle. Figure 31 shows a sample project milestones timeline.

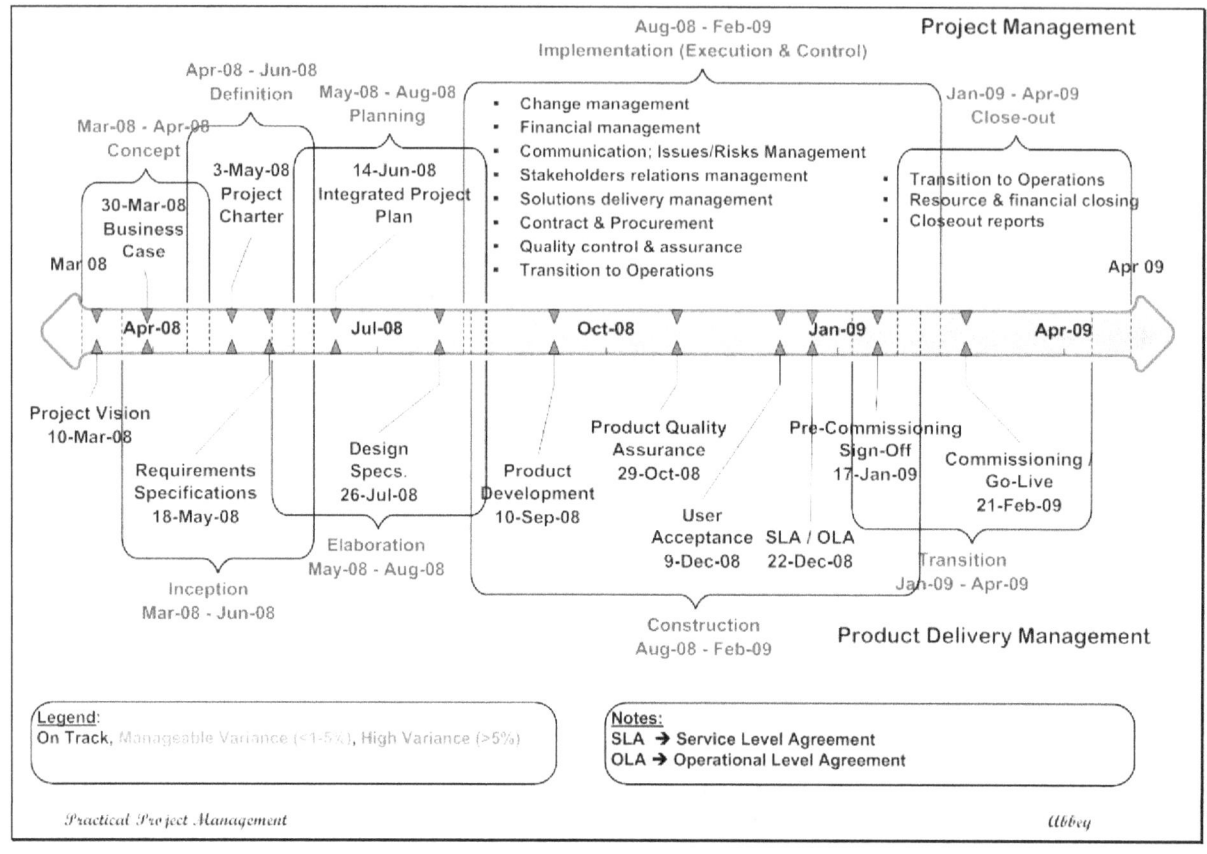

Figure 31 - Milestones Timeline

Table 10 - Milestones Timeline Template

PPMBook\DeliverResult\PPM_DeliveryTimeline.vsd

Table 10 includes a reference or link to a sample project milestones timeline template. This timeline is customizable. It was prepared using Microsoft® Visio. You may add legends and other attributes to provide a more descriptive content.

Team Formation and Kick-off Meeting(s)

Initial core team formation is a key prerequisite for the development of an integrated project plan and vital to running the project successfully. The resource requirements should be established as part of the project cost estimation and can be updated, due to other changing factors such as requirements scope and inflation.

Project team resources or members may be acquired internally and/or externally. External resources are acquired as consulting services via procurement process. Internal team resource could be obtained through the established resource sharing arrangement or negotiation with the resource managers or through the portfolio capacity planning exercise (the preferred method). Sometimes service, instead of resource, is procured to deliver part of the project or the entire project.

Once the core team members have been assigned and other stakeholders identified, you are ready to arrange and conduct the project kick-off meeting(s), with the goal of establishing a shared vision, common understanding of the project mandate and consequently developing the integrated project plan.

Key steps to a successful kick-off meeting include:

- Establish clear meeting agenda. The project charter, or project agenda/mandate in the absence of a formalized project charter, is a key input to the kick-off meeting. Information from the project charter should be extracted into a presentation format or the project agenda document.

- Identify and invite key participants.

- Provide coordination and facilitation to ensure orderliness and avoid derailment of the meeting to keep things on track.

- Brainstorm, analyze and decide. Separate ideas/options generation from analysis in order to take advantage of diverse and alternate ideas/options.

- Obtain agreements and ensure commitment to the project agenda/mandate.

- Document discussions, follow-up on action items and resolve issues/concerns.

- Communicate documentation and reports to participants.

- Obtain feedback and conduct follow-up sessions, if required.

Chapter 23 - Integrated Project Management Plan

"Everything should be made as simple as possible, but not simpler."   *Albert Einstein*

As shown in Figure 30 (Deliver Result - Key Steps, page 114), integrated project plan is made up of several plans in one. The integrated plan serves as the reference guide for the project manager and team members to manage and execute the project agenda. To create a comprehensive integrated project plan, you need the participations of the core project team and other key stakeholders. They help to identify and establish the key elements of the integrated project plan and provide the required commitments to implement the agreed plan.

Figure 32 shows a sample workflow that guides the creation, review, update, approvals and baseline of the integrated project plan. Once the project kick-off meeting has been successfully completed, the next key step is the project planning meeting(s).

Key steps to successful planning meeting(s), similar to the kick-off meeting, include:

- Establish clear meeting agenda. The project charter, or project agenda/mandate in the absence of a project charter, and the establishment of the core project team are prerequisites for conducting the project planning meeting(s).

- Identify and invite the key participants - the core project team and other stakeholders.

- Provide coordination and facilitation to ensure orderliness and avoid derailment of the meeting in order to keep things on track.

- Brainstorm, analyze and decide. Separate ideas/options generation from analysis in order to take advantage of diverse and alternate ideas/options.

- Obtain agreements from key stakeholders, particularly the core team, sponsor and champion, and ensure their commitments to the contents of the integrated project plan.

- Document discussions and inputs to create the plans.

- Communicate documentation and reports to participants. Follow-up on action items and resolve issues/concerns.

- Obtain feedback and conduct follow-up sessions, if required.

Integrated project plan is a comprehensive plan, which is required for the monitoring and controlling, executing and closing of the project. Integrated project plan could be prepared as a single document, and used as the authorized guide for end-to-end management of the project. However, for convenience, the plans can be kept as separate documents accompanied by a single index-type document for referencing the separate plans.

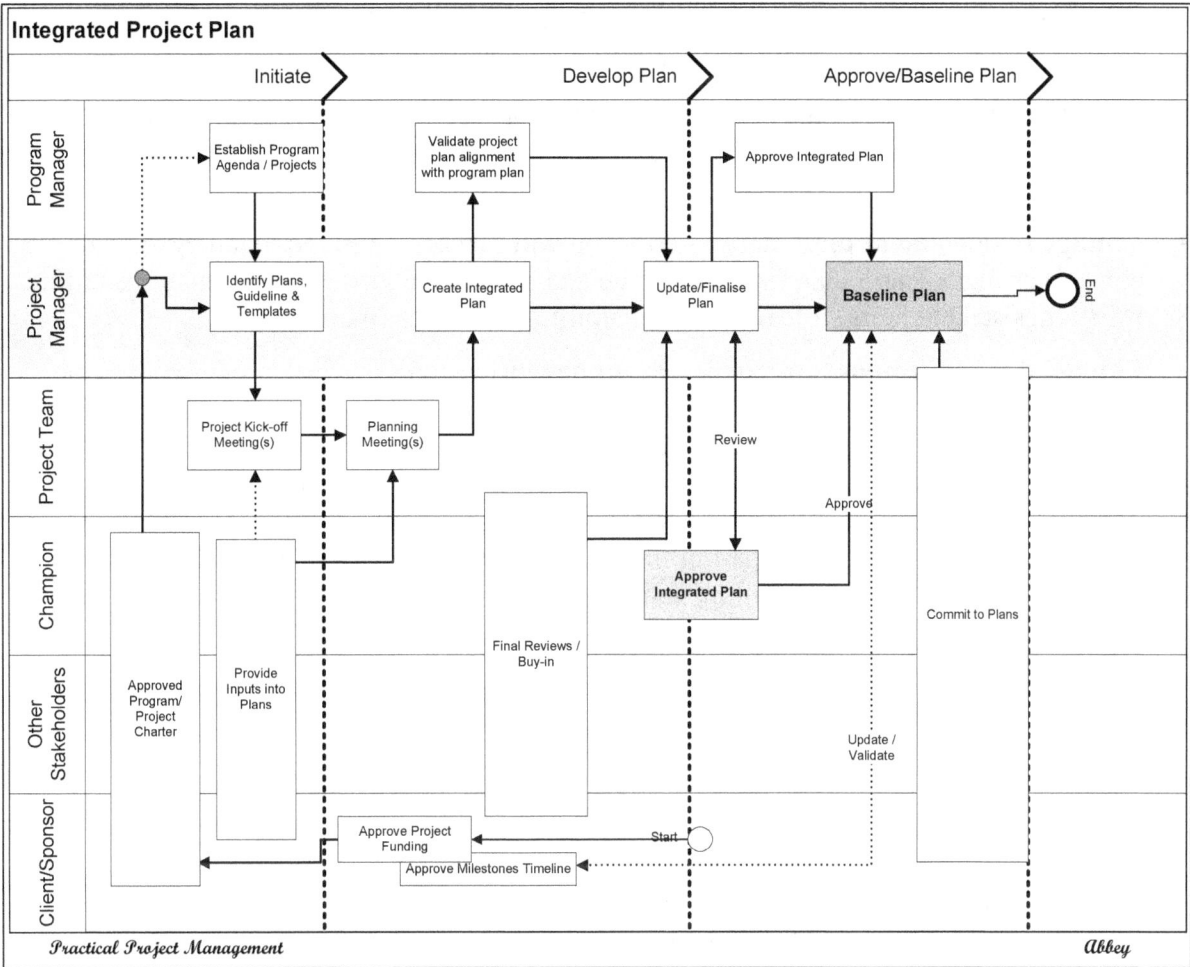

Figure 32 - Integrated Project Plan Workflow

The main elements of the integrated project plan include the following:

- **Scope management** (Deliverables / Work packages / WBS): work packages, usually expressed in a work breakdown structure, are the complete set of work components that need to be performed and completed to fulfill the desired project goals.

- **Time management** (project schedule): defines the work packages, activities, tasks, dependencies and resource assignment to ensure timely delivery of the work packages and associated deliverables.

- **Governance**: defines project organization structure and relationship, roles and responsibilities, and interfaces. It could be part of the communication plan.

- **Communication plan**: defines what, when and how information will be managed and shared with the stakeholders to ensure effective stakeholders, including project team, relationship management.

- **Risks management plan**: describes how risks will be identified, categorized, analyzed and mitigated; who will be involved and their roles, including the escalation procedure.

- **Stakeholders / human capital management plan**: defines human capital assignment matrix, availability and absence management, conflict resolution and stakeholder influence matrix (optional).

- **Change management plan**: defines how you will manage (respond to, analyze and control) changes, particularly scope change and its implications for cost, quality and time. It includes stakeholders' roles and responsibilities in change management.

- **Financial management / procurement management plan**: defines procurement plan that is applicable to your project needs. Consider your organization procurement policies and procedures, vendors' selection, request for information or proposal preparation, bid analysis, contract awards and administration guidelines. Define budget limits and associated delegation of authority to ensure fiscal responsibilities and include the financial approvals turn-around time as part of the planning process. Also, identify delivery and payment schedule, including billing and invoice payment process.

- **Quality management plan**: defines how to ensure the project deliver the product based on the agreed quality. It includes the guideline to ensure that the performance measures are controlled within the established performance thresholds.

- **Project interdependency plan**: identifies interdependencies between your project and other projects. It defines how to track and monitor interdependent activities to ensure that commitments between projects are fulfilled.

- You may adjust this list to reflect your organization standard. However, above list should suffice to enable you to effectively manage and deliver your project successfully.

Table 11 includes a reference or link to the integrated project plan template.

Table 11 - Integrated Project Plan Template

Template: PPMBook\DeliverResult\PPM_IntegratedProjectPlan.doc

Once an integrated project plan has been created, it should be base-lined and approved by the authorized person(s). Always re-baseline the plan, particularly the schedule, if the scope changed.

Work Packages (WBS)

Work breakdown structure (WBS) is a representation, usually in a chart or hierarchical form, of the work packages for a project. It defines the complete scope of the project. The subject matter experts collaborate to identify and define the components of the WBS. Effort should be geared towards achieving the desired outcome, which is determined by the successful and timely completion of the work packages and the associated deliverables. Avoid clouding your plan with irrelevancies and do not trivialize this part. When you are developing the WBS always ask the questions: Why is this work package or activity important? To which deliverable is this activity relevant?

Work breakdown structure (WBS) is a prerequisite for creating the project schedule. A very good tool for creating a WBS is the Mind Manager Pro (a mind mapping tool) or Microsoft® Project or their combination. My preferred method is to start with the Mind Manager Pro and migrate to Microsoft® Project to develop a comprehensive project schedule. WBS and schedule can be created in Mind Manager Pro, which provides the creative medium to brainstorm with the project team members. For example, this book was planned using the Mind Manager Pro to create the outline (a form of WBS), brainstorm ideas and develop the contents. A subset of the WBS for this book development is shown in Figure 33.

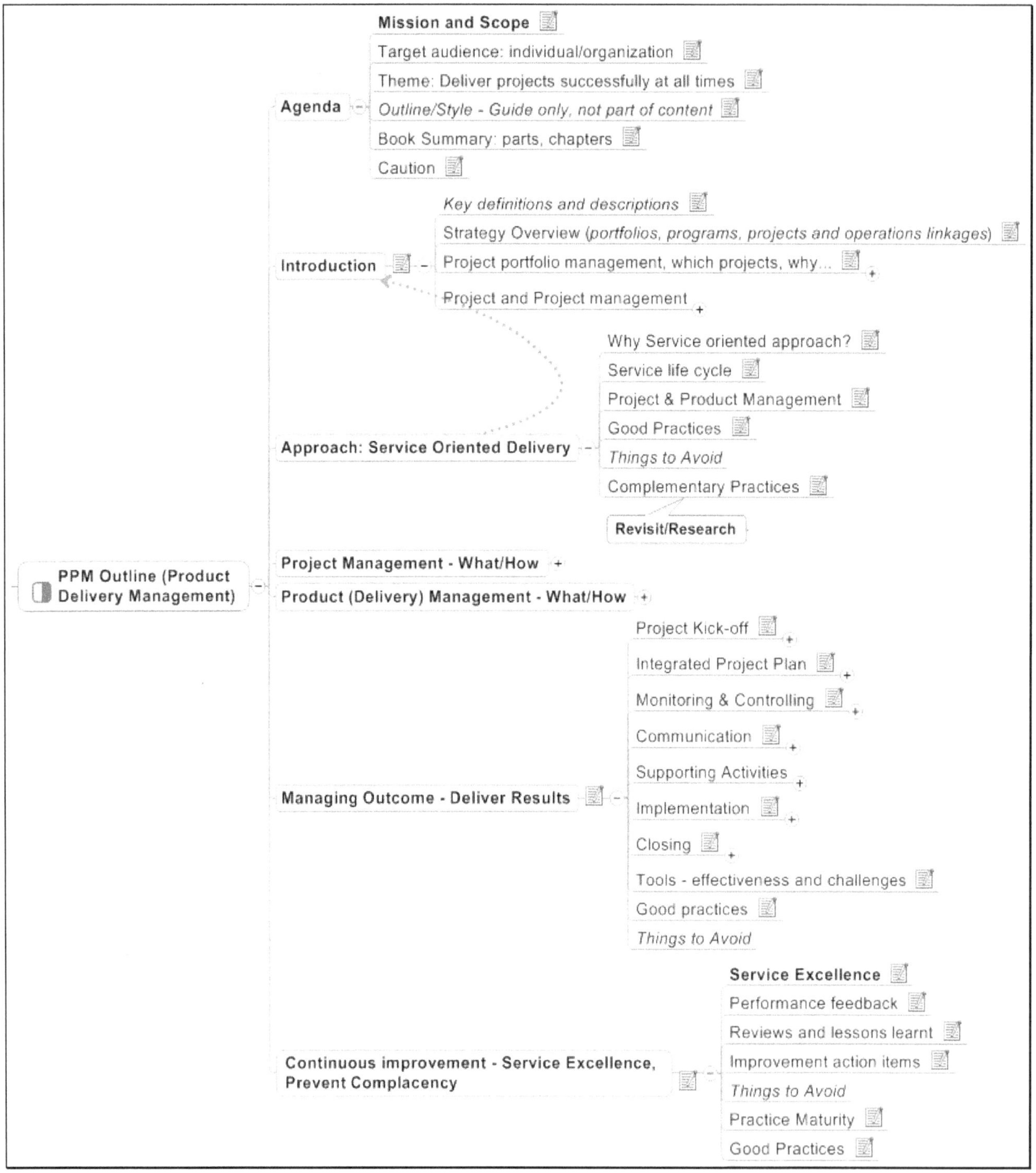

Mission and Scope

Target audience: individual/organization

Theme: Deliver projects successfully at all times

Outline/Style - Guide only, not part of content

Agenda

Book Summary: parts, chapters

Caution

Key definitions and descriptions

Strategy Overview *(portfolios, programs, projects and operations linkages)*

Introduction Project portfolio management, which projects, why...

Project and Project management

Why Service oriented approach?

Service life cycle

Project & Product Management

Good Practices

Approach: Service Oriented Delivery *Things to Avoid*

Complementary Practices

Revisit/Research

PPM Outline (Product Delivery Management)

Project Management - What/How

Product (Delivery) Management - What/How

Project Kick-off

Integrated Project Plan

Monitoring & Controlling

Communication

Supporting Activities

Managing Outcome - Deliver Results Implementation

Closing

Tools - effectiveness and challenges

Good practices

Things to Avoid

Service Excellence

Performance feedback

Reviews and lessons learnt

Improvement action items

Continuous improvement - Service Excellence, Prevent Complacency *Things to Avoid*

Practice Maturity

Good Practices

Figure 33 - Work Breakdown Structure

Project Schedule

Once the key work packages, deliverables and milestones have been defined, project schedule can be created. Project schedule include activities, tasks and their dependencies, resource information and resource assignments. Project schedule can be prepared in different format and levels to represent clear point of responsibility. Keep it simple and understandable by each lead or the assigned resource. Each activity and associated deliverable should have a single point of responsibility. Going into too much details to define tasks, may not be necessary. Do it to a point at which an assignment or responsibility can be defined.

Once the project schedule has been completed, updated, approved and base-lined, the schedule milestones information should be kept in sync with the milestones timeline. Focus your attention on the deliverables and the desired outcome, look ahead and watch for signals (threats and opportunities) and respond appropriately. Every effort should be geared towards the successful completion of the deliverables and the desired outcome.

The key components of a project schedule include:

- Gantt chart: includes activities and tasks by process group or phase, start and end dates, deliverables, dependencies, and the project critical path that needs to be watched at all times to anticipate any slippage in the project schedule.

- Resource schedule: includes resource name, type, availability and rate.

Figure 34 shows a sample project schedule, the Gantt chart, created using Microsoft® Project.

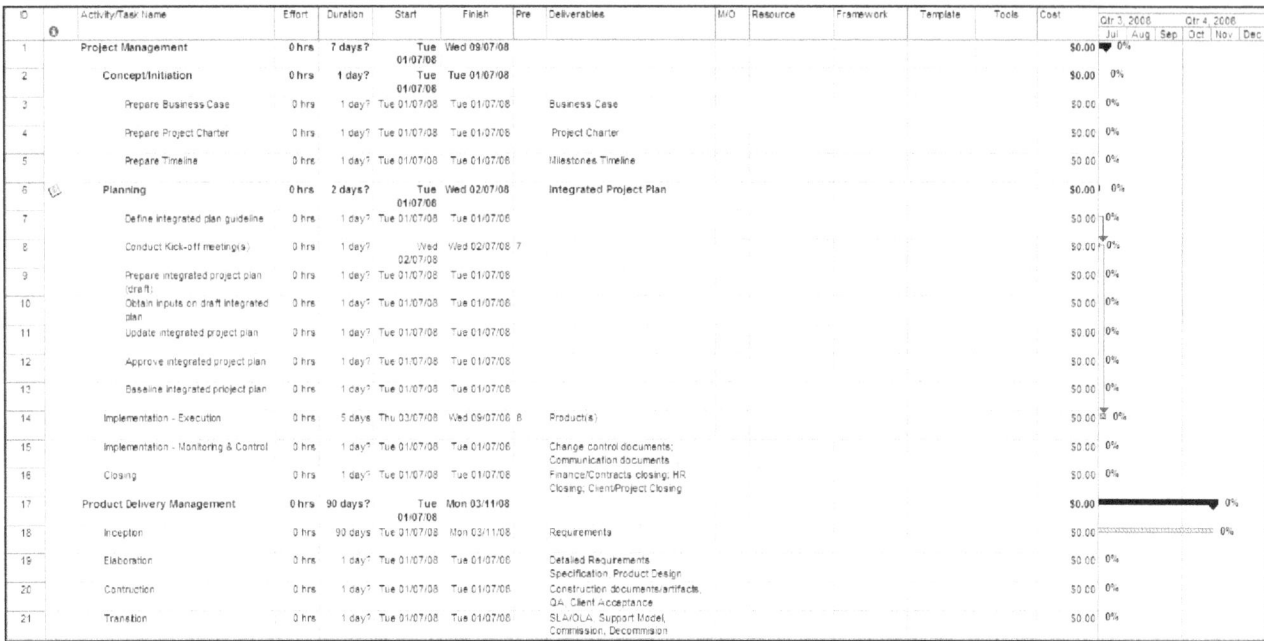

ID		Activity/Task Name	Effort	Duration	Start	Finish	Pre	Deliverables	M/O	Resource	Framework	Template	Tools	Cost	Qtr 3, 2008 Jul Aug Sep	Qtr 4, 2008 Oct Nov Dec
1		Project Management	0 hrs	7 days?	Tue 01/07/08	Wed 09/07/08								$0.00	0%	
2		Concept/Initiation	0 hrs	1 day?	Tue 01/07/08	Tue 01/07/08								$0.00	0%	
3		Prepare Business Case	0 hrs	1 day?	Tue 01/07/08	Tue 01/07/08		Business Case						$0.00	0%	
4		Prepare Project Charter	0 hrs	1 day?	Tue 01/07/08	Tue 01/07/08		Project Charter						$0.00	0%	
5		Prepare Timeline	0 hrs	1 day?	Tue 01/07/08	Tue 01/07/08		Milestones Timeline						$0.00	0%	
6		Planning	0 hrs	2 days?	Tue 01/07/08	Wed 02/07/08		Integrated Project Plan						$0.00	0%	
7		Define integrated plan guideline	0 hrs	1 day?	Tue 01/07/08	Tue 01/07/08								$0.00	0%	
8		Conduct Kick-off meeting(s)	0 hrs	1 day?	Wed 02/07/08	Wed 02/07/08	7							$0.00	0%	
9		Prepare integrated project plan (draft)	0 hrs	1 day?	Tue 01/07/08	Tue 01/07/08								$0.00	0%	
10		Obtain inputs on draft integrated plan	0 hrs	1 day?	Tue 01/07/08	Tue 01/07/08								$0.00	0%	
11		Update integrated project plan	0 hrs	1 day?	Tue 01/07/08	Tue 01/07/08								$0.00	0%	
12		Approve integrated project plan	0 hrs	1 day?	Tue 01/07/08	Tue 01/07/08								$0.00	0%	
13		Baseline integrated project plan	0 hrs	1 day?	Tue 01/07/08	Tue 01/07/08								$0.00	0%	
14		Implementation - Execution	0 hrs	5 days	Thu 03/07/08	Wed 09/07/08	8	Product(s)						$0.00	0%	
15		Implementation - Monitoring & Control	0 hrs	1 day?	Tue 01/07/08	Tue 01/07/08		Change control documents; Communication documents						$0.00	0%	
16		Closing	0 hrs	1 day?	Tue 01/07/08	Tue 01/07/08		Finance/Contracts closing; HR Closing; Client/Project Closing						$0.00	0%	
17		Product Delivery Management	0 hrs	90 days?	Tue 01/07/08	Mon 03/11/08								$0.00	0%	
18		Inception	0 hrs	90 days	Tue 01/07/08	Mon 03/11/08		Requirements						$0.00	0%	
19		Elaboration	0 hrs	1 day?	Tue 01/07/08	Tue 01/07/08		Detailed Requirements Specification, Product Design						$0.00	0%	
20		Construction	0 hrs	1 day?	Tue 01/07/08	Tue 01/07/08		Construction documents/artifacts, QA, Client Acceptance						$0.00	0%	
21		Transition	0 hrs	1 day?	Tue 01/07/08	Tue 01/07/08		SLA/OLA, Support Model, Commission, Decommission						$0.00	0%	

Figure 34 - Sample Project Schedule

Notes on abbreviated columns:
Pre => Predecessor
MO => Mandatory/Optional

Communication - Governance

'The primary safeguards against abuses of power in an organization are character, humility and judgement'[6].

Strategic governance is critical to successful project management. It is the last resort to resolving unresolved issues, particularly roles and responsibilities, at every organizational level. Governance is vital to ensure well defined roles and responsibilities, leadership discipline, exercise some level of control and provide support to ensure project success. A practical project governance model is show in Figure 35. In most cases, the sponsor or his/her delegate leads the steering committee.

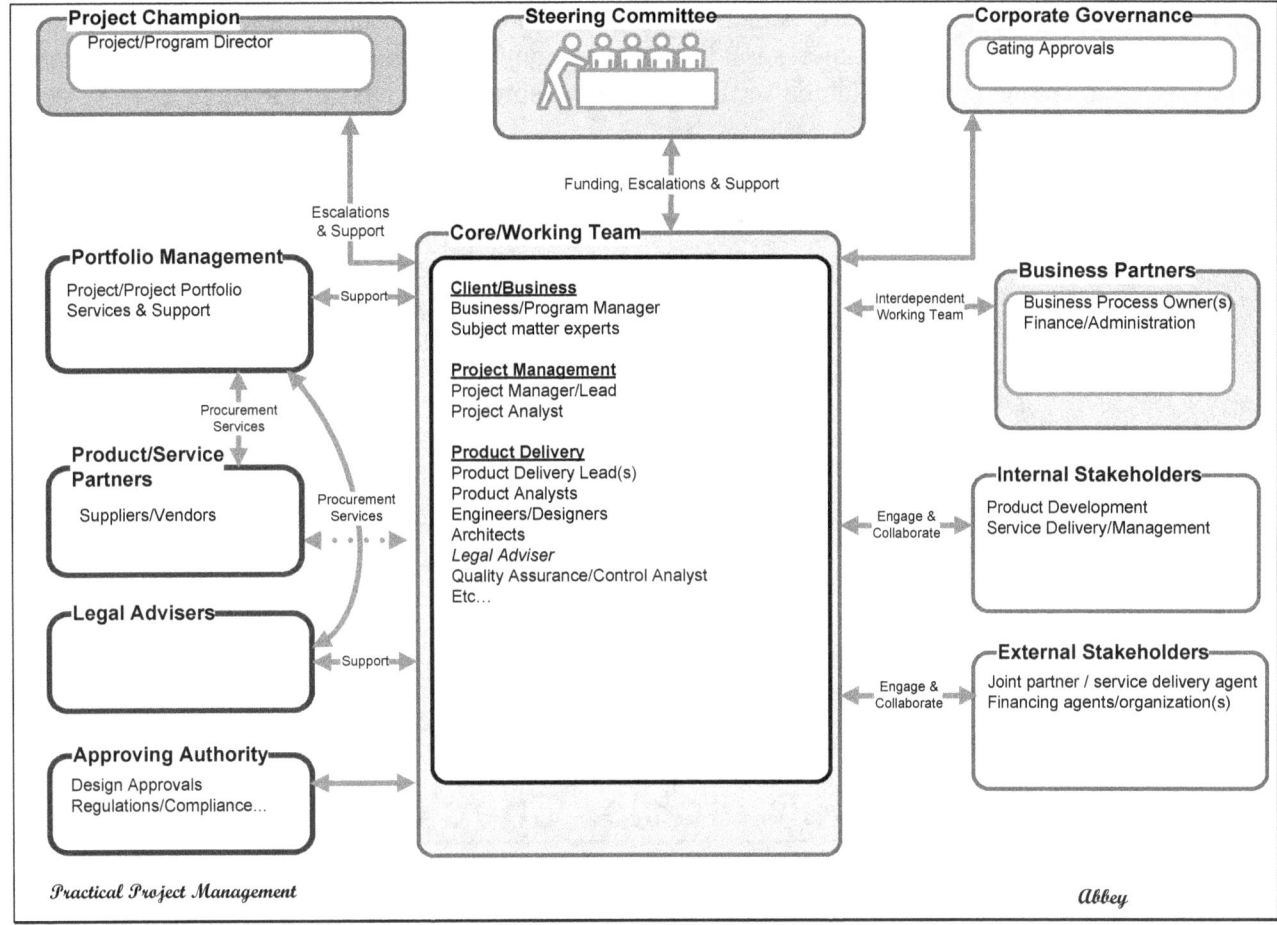

Figure 35 - Project Governance

Take note of the following regarding project governance:

- Organization culture that does not comprehend, practice or have the leadership discipline of project management, usually undervalue the role of a project manager. A project manager may have some challenges in this type of organization. However, you can still deliver successful projects through your effective leadership, courage and good judgment. Though it could be sometime at a cost to you; regardless, you have to make your choice. You need to weigh your options - to be more of a professional and less political or become a push over.

- As a project manager, regardless of the organization culture, encourage the executives to acknowledge the formal establishment of governance for each project. It should be clearly defined and respected to facilitate an effective project team (high relationship and high result team).

- Have clearly defined responsibilities for the sponsor, the champion (an industry enthusiast or 'god-father') and the steering committee. The steering committee helps to create a green field and settled water to ensure the success of the project.

Projects Interdependency

There could be interdependencies between your project and other projects within and outside the organization, or between your project and others within a large project or program. It is important to identify the interdependencies between projects to determine their impacts on your project and your project impacts on them.

Establishing projects interdependency enables you to understand and focus on your primary responsibilities and identify areas not under your control where you need help from, that is other projects or projects' activities you depend on to complete your assignment. Projects interdependency will be discussed further in the later section (see Figure 41, page 140). Table 12 includes a reference or link to the projects interdependency template.

Table 12 - Project Delivery Interface Template

PPMBook\DeliverResult\PPM_ProjectDeliveryInteface.doc

Deliverables Checklist

Deliverables checklist provides a quick overview of the project deliverables, which can be used as a tracking tool. It may also include the key responsible and accountable parties to ensure timely completion of the deliverables or to achieve the milestones. Maintaining one comprehensive checklist, for tracking, enables the project manager to be on top of the key activities, deliverables and emerging issues.

A checklist can be organized or categorized by project management and product delivery management process groups. You can track the project progress using the checklist and the milestones timeline. You may drill down, using the project schedule, to track details, particularly when you detect signals or control thresholds which may impact project delivery time, cost or quality. A concise checklist for tracking the deliverables or milestones completion, responsibility and accountability, including the delegation of authority, is critical to staying focus and on track. Table 13 includes a reference or link to the project control checklist template.

Table 13 - Project Control Checklist Template

PPMBook\DeliverResult\PPM_ProjectControlChecklist.doc

Chapter 24 - Monitoring and Controlling

"Trust but verify."   *Ronald Reagan*

Monitor key outcomes and deliverables at established intervals as agreed with the lead or focal point for each assignment. Every commitment has to be monitored, tracked and controlled to ensure that performances are within approved and agreed limits. It is the sole duty of the project manager to ensure that all targets are met, at the agreed cost, quality and time.

A seasoned project manager will focus his/her attention on results. He/she chases the outcome, not every micro task, and helps remove obstacles (by him/herself or through others) to ensure that outcomes are delivered on time and on budget, and meet the desired quality; hold others responsible and/or accountable for all assignments. Focusing your attention on every task will distract you from aiming at the target and the outcome. However, be aware, track and respond swiftly to tasks and dependencies, particularly those on the critical path, that may become bottlenecks to other tasks and the project.

Aim before you shoot. Wasting ammunition is like wasting time, effort and money. Therefore, aim wisely and shoot with the end in mind. Focus on the first thing first in order to avoid zigzag movement, which lead to more time wasting. Your path may not be smooth, but do not make it rougher by your actions or inactions.

The following elements and work components should be monitored and controlled in a timely fashion:

- **Project scope** and associated change requests.

- **Project schedule** - progress/status of the project activities, tasks and associated deliverables; and any change that may impact the schedule, which may require re-baseline.

- **Cost control** - is vital to ensuring that cost is kept within the budget limit. All cost escalations should be monitored and controlled in a timely fashion. Cost escalations may be due to change in scope, change in contract cost due to exogenous risk factors and inflation. Project cost outlay or expenditure should be tracked based on the measurable target deliverables, identify discrepancies to predict cost projections and possible cost overrun or under-spent.

- **Issues and Risks** - tracking, mitigation and resolution. Track issues and risks identification, resolution and mitigation, to ensure that they do not negatively impact the desired project outcome.

- **Quality Control** - every aspect of the project management and product delivery management should be monitored and controlled to ensure that the desired quality is achieved and performances are kept within acceptable thresholds (specified and agreed with the sponsor or client designate).

- **Stakeholders,** including human resource - establish participative objectives and performance targets, and obtain stakeholders' commitments; track performance, control and resolve conflicts.

- **Procurement/Contract administration** - includes request for information, request for service, request for proposal, contract administration, suppliers' relationship management, receipts of goods and services, invoicing and payments.

- **Projects interdependencies** - fulfill your commitments to other projects that depend on your project deliverables or outcome. Collaborate and follow up to obtain other projects' (or sources') deliverables upon which your project depends to succeed. If possible, attend other projects' key status meetings or review their status reports.

Additional information will be provided on the above key elements in the subsequent sections. Figure 36 shows a project change control management workflow. Like issues and risks, track all changes in a change log. A change log could be a shared document or a repository within an enterprise project management system.

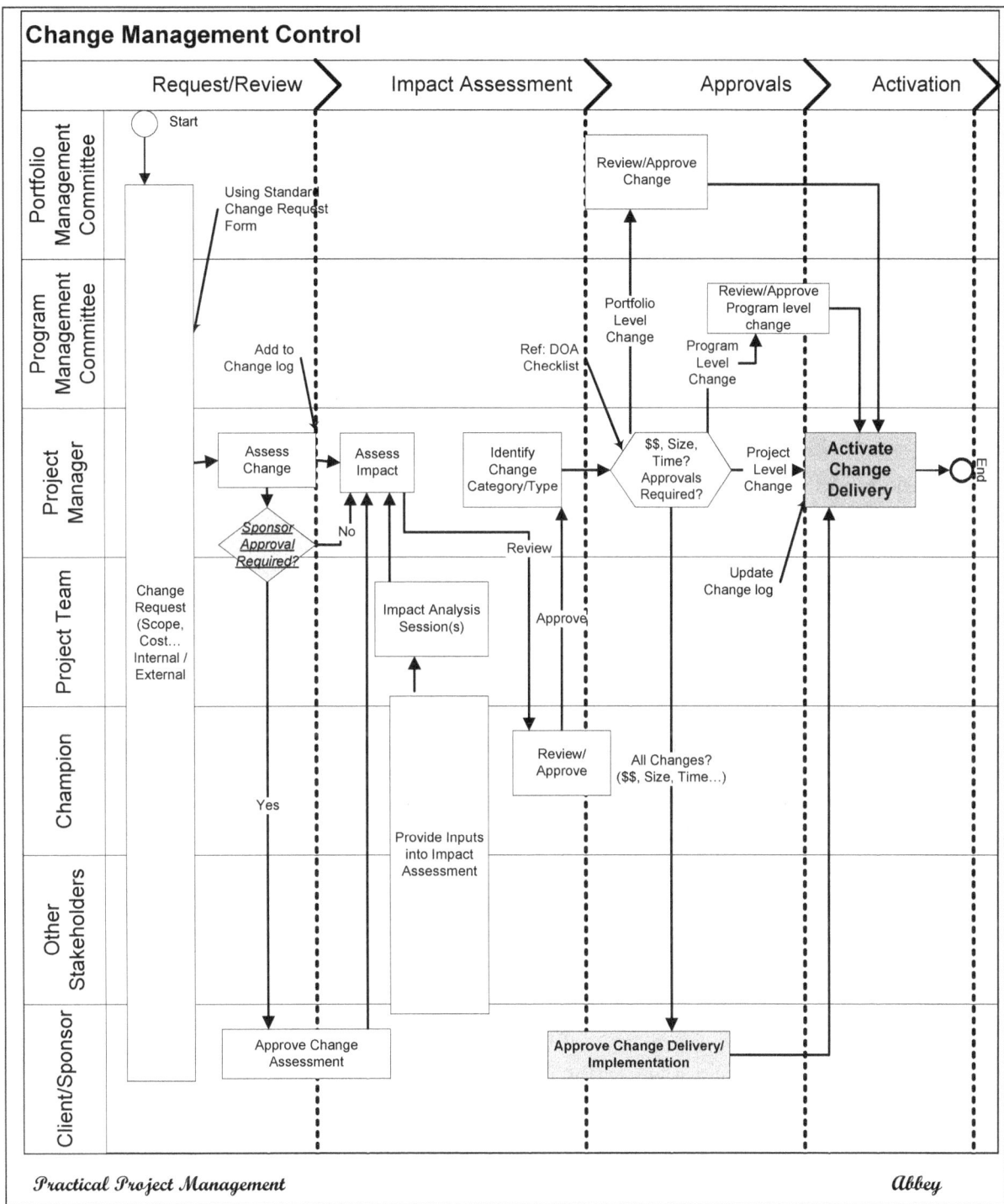

Figure 36 - Project Change Control Management Workflow

Chapter 25 - Communication

"Writing without thinking is like shooting without aiming."   *Arnold Glasgow*

Communicating effectively is something you have to adjust to, because not everyone will interpret your message in the same way it was intended and each organization has its own idiosyncrasy. It takes practice to perfect your communication acts. Therefore, be prepared to explain, repeat, rephrase and re-present your messages, as may be required.

Communicating effectively requires experience, ability to understand, good judgement, establishment of the right processes and tools (systems, information format and exchange), and engaging the stakeholders appropriately and on time.

Ensure information quality by creating single source of the same information at all times. Limit the number of reports you produce; produce relevant reports that are needed and used by the stakeholders. You may organize your reports into groups, this way you produce limited quality reports that can be used and referenced separately by different stakeholder groups.

Avoid information overload*.* Information overload could create information fatigue, which explains why most messages are not read or referenced, except in critical situations. It is important that the project manager ensures documentation of all project related information and share them with the relevant parties. However, this should be kept as simple and precise as possible, perfection is not the goal, rather it is the creation and sharing of relevant information or messages that count.

Caution about reporting: manual process could be tedious, automated tool is preferred but will not solve all communication problems. Efficient and effective reports are created through sound practice and discipline by the stakeholders. ***Data quality is a major prerequisite to producing quality report****.* Data quality should be part of any serious organization's culture. Any organization that pays lip service to data quality (that is, clear data definition, custodian or ownership, supplier, storage and frequency of update), usually struggle with making the right decision or make decision based on guess work or manipulated report that was based on ambiguous data. Paying lip service to data quality is a recipe for disaster, confusion and frustration.

Figure 37 shows a project communication management framework. It shows the key players, their interactions, information flow and supporting systems or tools.

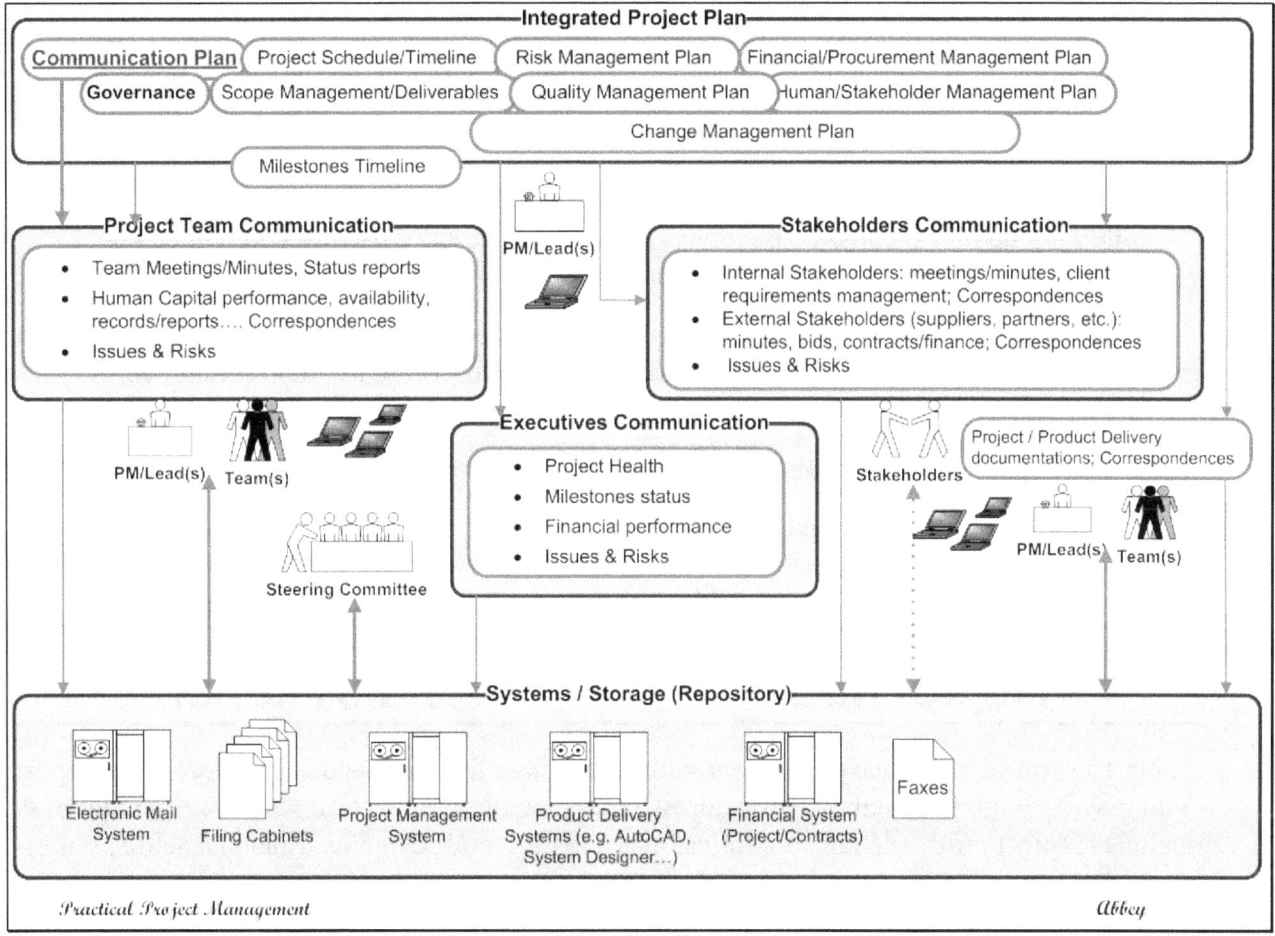

Figure 37 - Project Communication Management

Project Team Minutes and Status Report

Effective communication is critical to making your team fully engaged and becoming a performing team. Key steps to effective team communication include:

- ***Conduct regular team meetings*** for status review, issues and risks monitoring, conflict and problem resolutions, team building etc. Establish clear agenda and avoid trying to discuss and resolve all issues in a single meeting. Keep the meeting within a specific time range, preferably short.

- ***Be a positive influence, motivator and role model*** in leading by examples, showing good judgement, willing and volunteering to go above and beyond.

- *Organize your thoughts*, your correspondences, documentation etc.

- *Minutes and status for core project team* - keeping your team informed and on the same page, promoting complementary team work and bringing issues to the open facilitate the successful delivery of your projects. Be sensitive to managing confidential issues that you may not want to include in the general team report.

- *Interact with your team members, sometimes informally*, not just when you are following up on expected deliverables, activities or tasks. This way you will be able to create a relax or less stressed atmosphere.

- *Good practice* - prepare and send your minutes of meetings on the same day (preferred) or within 24 hours of the meeting. This way you are able to capture the meeting events clearly without loosing key points and details, and keep action items on track.

Table 14 includes a reference or link to a project team report/minutes template.

Table 14 - Project Team Report/Minutes Template

PPMBook\DeliverResult\PPM_ProjectTeamReportMinutes.doc

Project Health – Executive Status Report

Table 15 shows a reference or link to a sample template for the executive project status report. You may customize the template to address your specific organization's needs. Essentially, it includes project profile and health, milestones and deliverables status, financial status, issues and risks.

Table 15 - Executive Project Status Report Template

PPMBook\DeliverResult\PPM_ExecutiveProjectStatusReport.doc

Prepare and present project information and reports to the executive in the following order:

- High level - this is very important, if they trust and respect your judgement as a professional and proven based on past experiences. You may stay at this level with the executives.

- Summary breakdown - is required to support the high level presentation, to clarify and answer questions.

- Details - you will not be at this level with the executives, except in rare cases, where key signals and issues force them to drill down. However, this is rare but possible.

Prepare yourself, with relevant information, to respond to queries on your project performance. If you do not have the required information, do not waver or try to 'play smart'.

The preferred approach is to be honest and request for time to obtain additional information as may be required. Result oriented executives, though need you to act proactively, swiftly and rightly, want you to succeed.

Correspondences and Documentation

Besides project team and executive reports, similar reports may be created for other stakeholder groups to keep them informed, thus ensuring that nothing fall through the crack and timely responses are provided to resolving emerging issues, risks and conflicts. Other reports may include contract performance reports to track the suppliers' performance. Figure 16 (page 77) shows a sample work organization structure that could be used or customized to organize your correspondences and documentation, to ensure easy and timely access to information.

Chapter 26 - Supporting Activities

Issues and Risks Management

Whatever you do, always pay considerable attention to issues and risks management. Engage all the key stakeholders in issues/risks identification, developing mitigation and resolution strategies to respond to the identified risks and issues. Maintain a log to track issues and risks, as part of the team meeting, status and performance reports. If your organization has an enterprise system to capture issues and risks, make use of it. Enterprise system provides excellent assignment, tracking and follow up mechanism; for example, using email alert or workflow.

Tip: record all issues and risks as they occur in the minutes of meeting or issue/risk log. Allocate about 30 minutes per week, or 10 minutes per day, to record them in a central system, accessible to all stakeholders. Manage issues and risks as you manage other project activities; that is, they must have owners, target resolution date, status update and outcome.

Unresolved issues and risks, at the team level, should be escalated and reflected in the executive report. There is no point reporting all issues and risks to the executives, except the escalated or unresolved ones which are impacting the project health. Providing relevant and timely information on issues and risks will focus the executives' attention on the impact and enable them to provide the required support to get the issues resolved.

Issues and risks logs may be created for different groups, especially if you have sub-projects within a large project or a program. For instance, you may maintain separate issue/risk logs for the third party work packages to ensure effective tracking and focus. Figure 38 shows a typical issues and risks management framework, which can be customized for your use. It shows the key steps, stakeholders and applicable systems or tools.

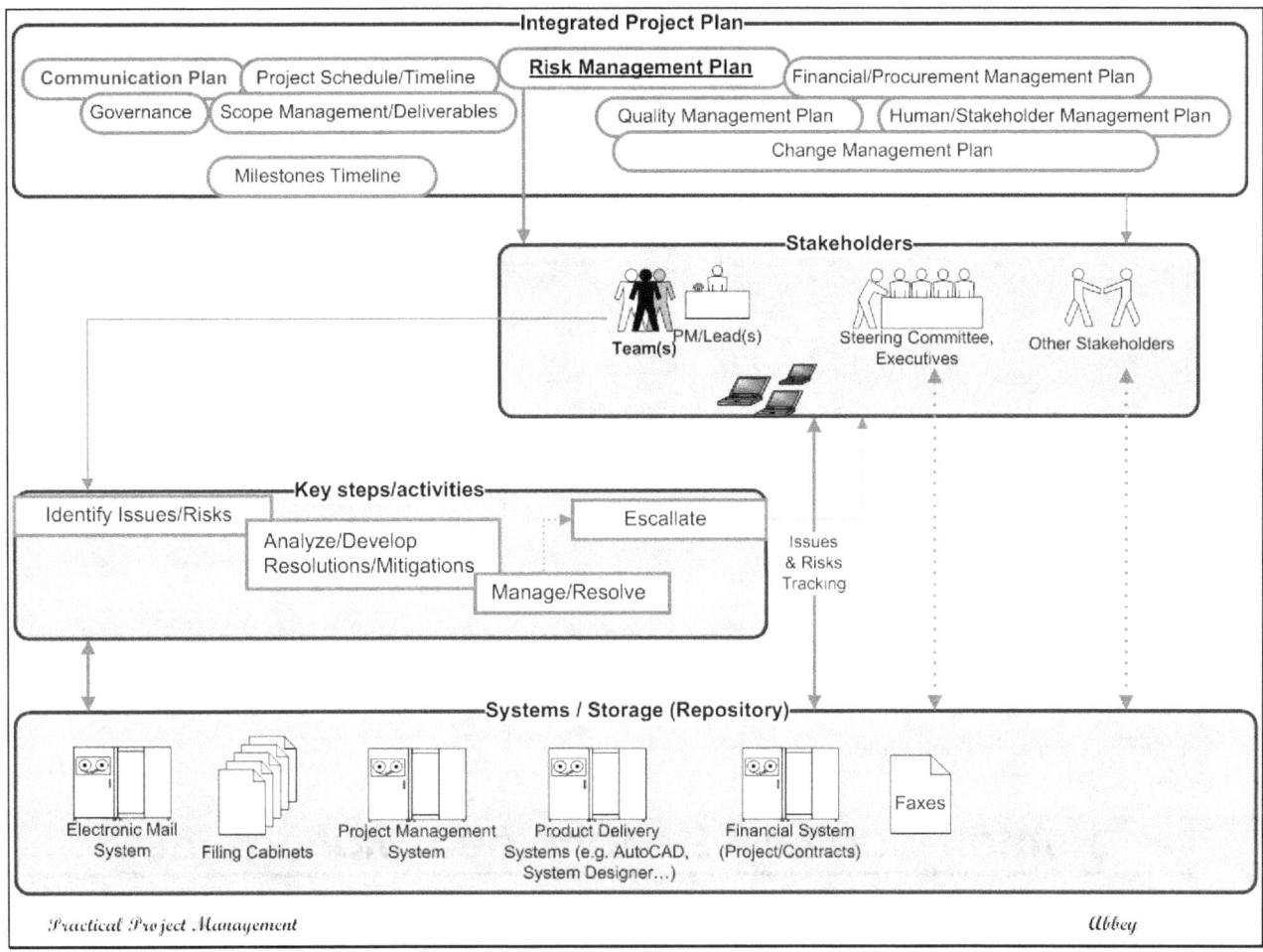

Figure 38 - Issues & Risks Management

Procurement / Contract Management

The procurement process, activities and key players are discussed in Part 4 (Project Management). Figure 39 shows a repeat of the procurement framework, which you may find handy.

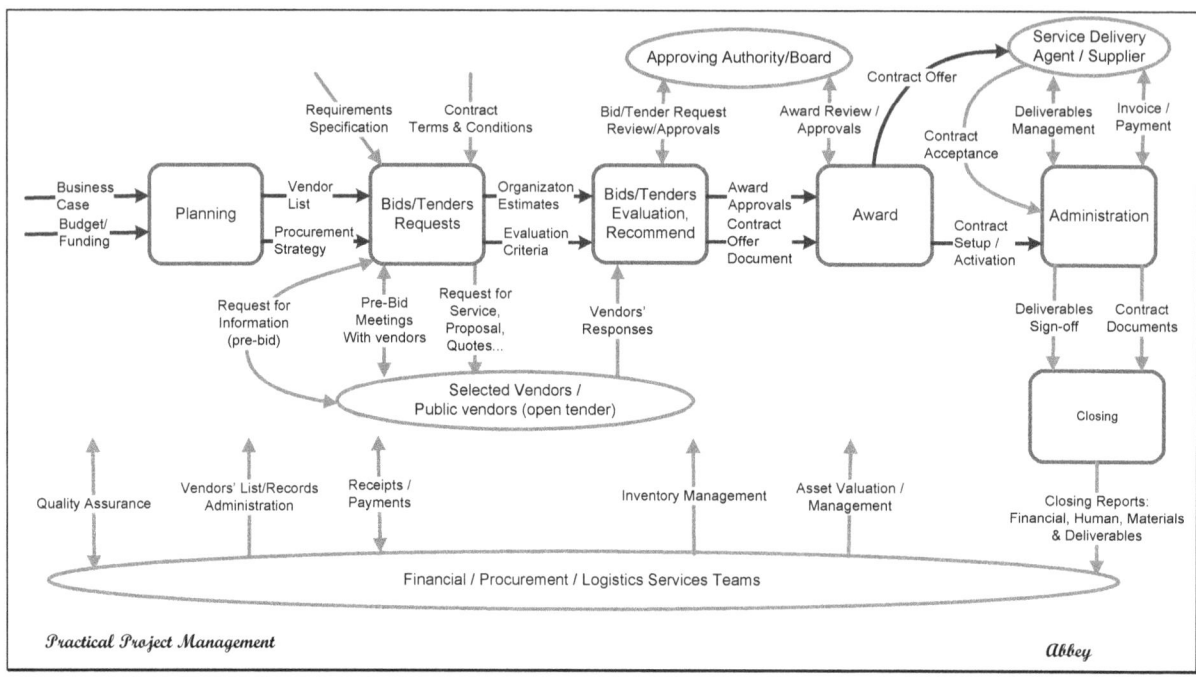

Figure 39 - Procurement Guide (reference)

Human Capital / Stakeholders Management

At the centre of effective human capital and stakeholders management is **communication**. You relate with the project team members and other stakeholders (sponsor, champion, steering committee, internal and external partners, including goods and service providers) at different stages of the project management life cycle.

The main focus of human capital management includes the following:

- Engage the team and other stakeholders to be a high performing team, through team building, providing timely support, create green field for team success, regularly follow-up on action items and report status updates.

- Ensure commitments are fulfilled by various action parties.

- Track, control and resolve conflicts in a timely fashion.

- Manage availability and absences, as they affect delivery dates.

Figure 40 (human capital and stakeholders management framework) shows the interactions between the stakeholders, activities and applicable systems.

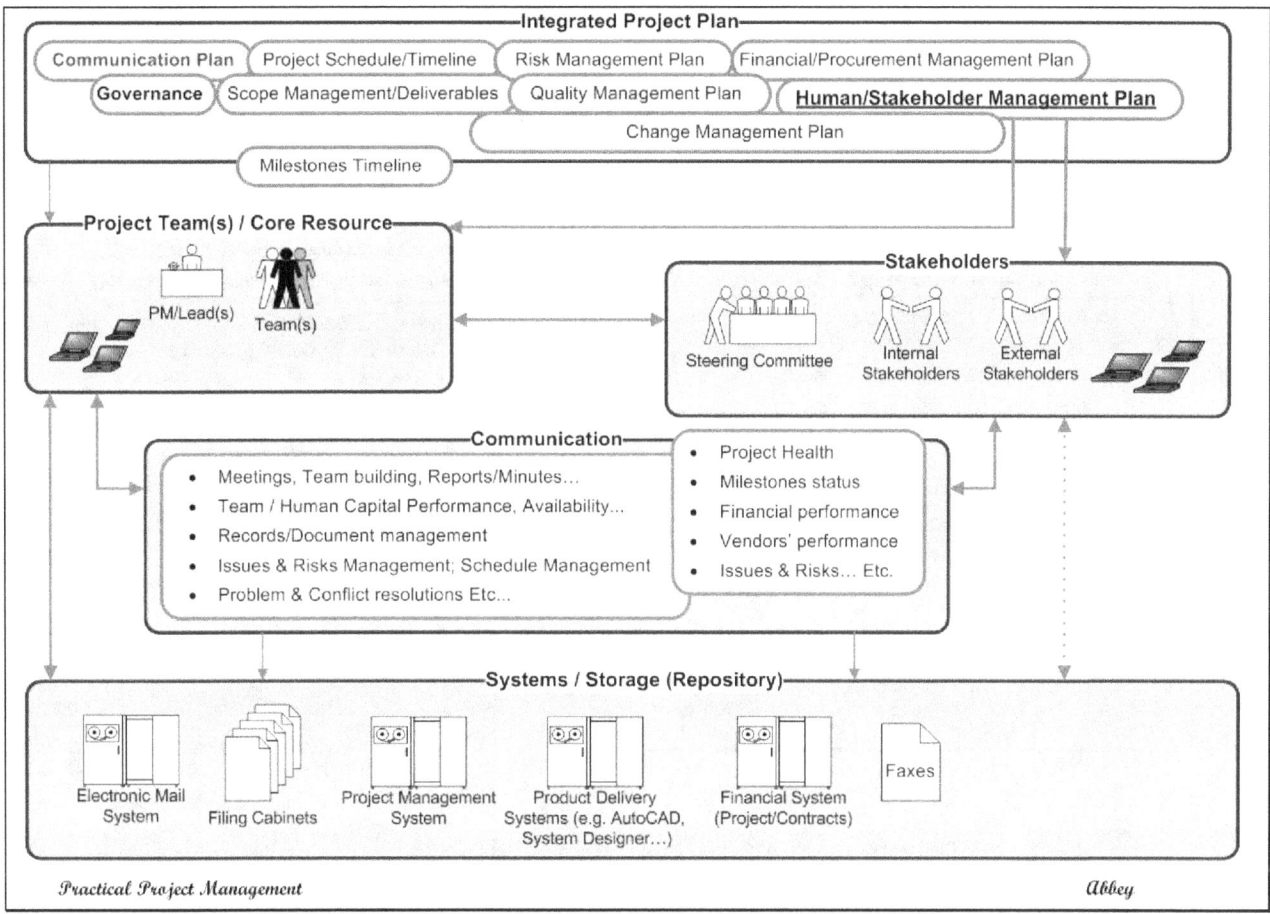

Figure 40 - Human Capital and Stakeholders Management

Projects Interdependency

Further to the previous discussion on projects interdependency, Figure 41 shows the representation of the interdependencies between your project and other projects within and outside the organization. You need to fulfill your project commitment to other projects and follow-up on obtaining responses from other projects that your project success depends upon. Ensure that there is a single point of contact for each project in the dependency zones.

Table 16 includes a reference or link to a project interface document template.

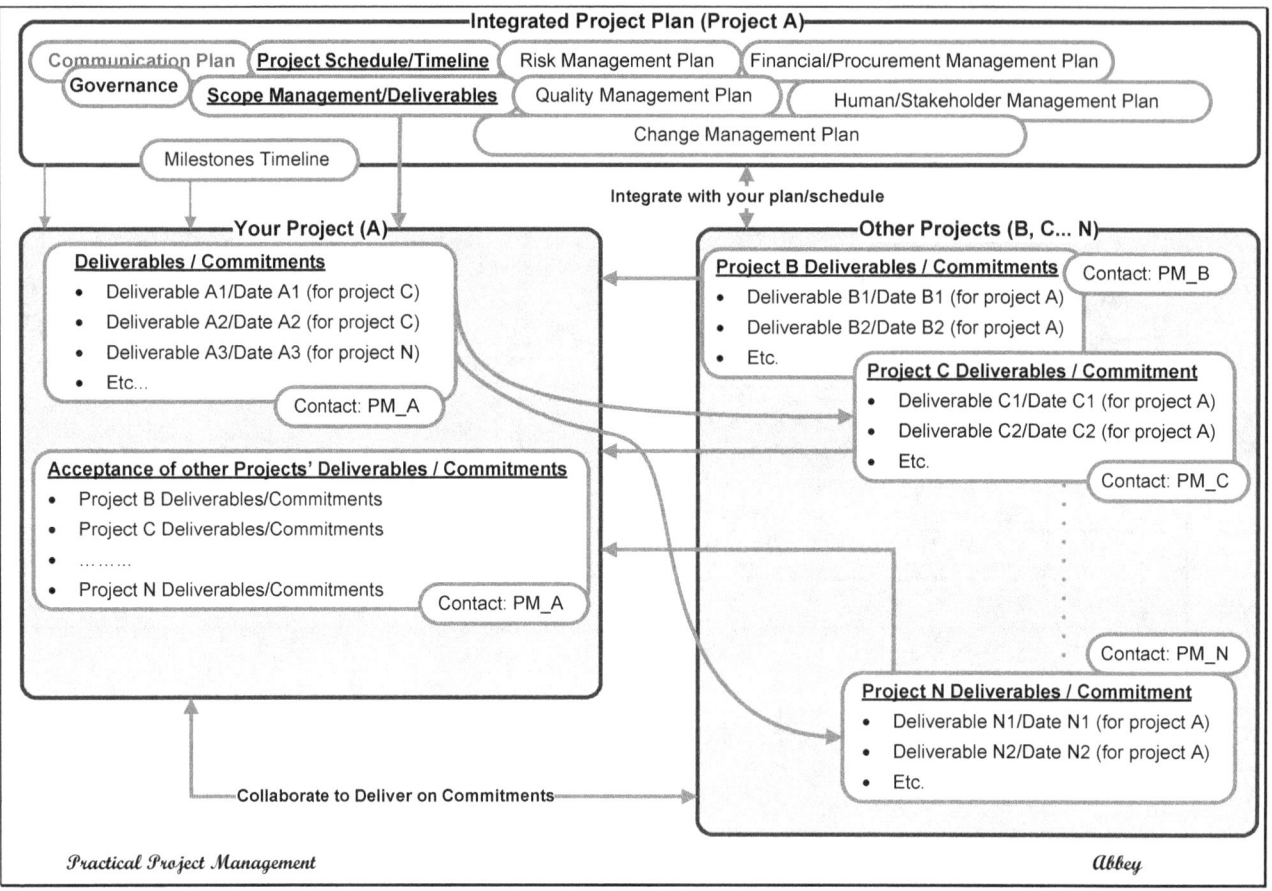

Figure 41 - Project Dependency

Table 16 - Project Interface Document Template

PPMBook\ProjectManagement\ PPM_ProjectInterface.doc

Soft Skills and Issues Management

Key soft skills have been discussed in Part 4 (Project Management). Effective application of soft skills (for examples, influencing and political awareness) will have positive impact on your project outcome. Furthermore, take note of the following, though they may seem obvious but worth emphasizing:

- Regardless of what you do you may not be able to please everyone; however, pleasing most people is better than displeasing few people. You goal is to meet all expectations.

- Stay calm, thoughtful and act swiftly to project events. Your actions should not be creating a new problem, which may cost you more time and money to resolve. The more the problems you have to deal with, the more time you will spend on resolving them, further delaying your project and costing more money. You will always save time doing due diligence in planning your course of action.

- It is your duty, as a project manager, to track, monitor and control project activities, and ask for update from the participating stakeholders no matter their levels. Every stakeholder is responsible to one another. The sponsor is responsible for providing the funding and support, the project team is responsible for the project deliverables and fulfilling client expectations.

- Recognize the impact of each stakeholder on the project. Keep them informed, seek their support and manage their expectations.

- Mind your language, particularly your body language or posture. Open (friendly, but sometimes firm) posture is preferred to close (unfriendly or intimidating) gesture. Close posture promotes passive response and argument, which usually lead to deadlock. Open gesture promotes interactive debate, which leads to result.

Chapter 27 - Implementation

This is the execution phase to complete the project deliverables and accomplish the project goals. The deliverables require the completion of work packages. A work package consists of activities and tasks. Usually a lead or a subject matter expert is responsible for completing specific work packages and the associated deliverables. In order to ensure an unbiased judgement regarding the quality assurance of the product, sometimes an independent subject matter expert is responsible for the quality of the deliverables and of the final product.

The completion of all the work packages and the associated deliverables fulfill the project outcome and goals. All deliverables are tested to ensure quality assurance. A client approval that may be based on recommendation report from the quality assurance expert is required prior to going live or commissioning of the new product or service.

Figure 42 (Deliver Result - Implementation, page 143) shows the implementation framework. The main focus of the implementation is to deliver the desired product that will meet the client needs. It includes the following process groups, processes and components:

- **Product delivery management** - includes requirements, analysis, design, construction, quality assurance, client acceptance and transition to operation (commissioning/ commercialization) processes.

- **Request for change management** for assessing the impact of introducing new product in an existing environment and deciding on the change implementation, usually by approving authority within and/or outside the organization.

- **Operational and Service level agreements** to sustain the new or changed product.

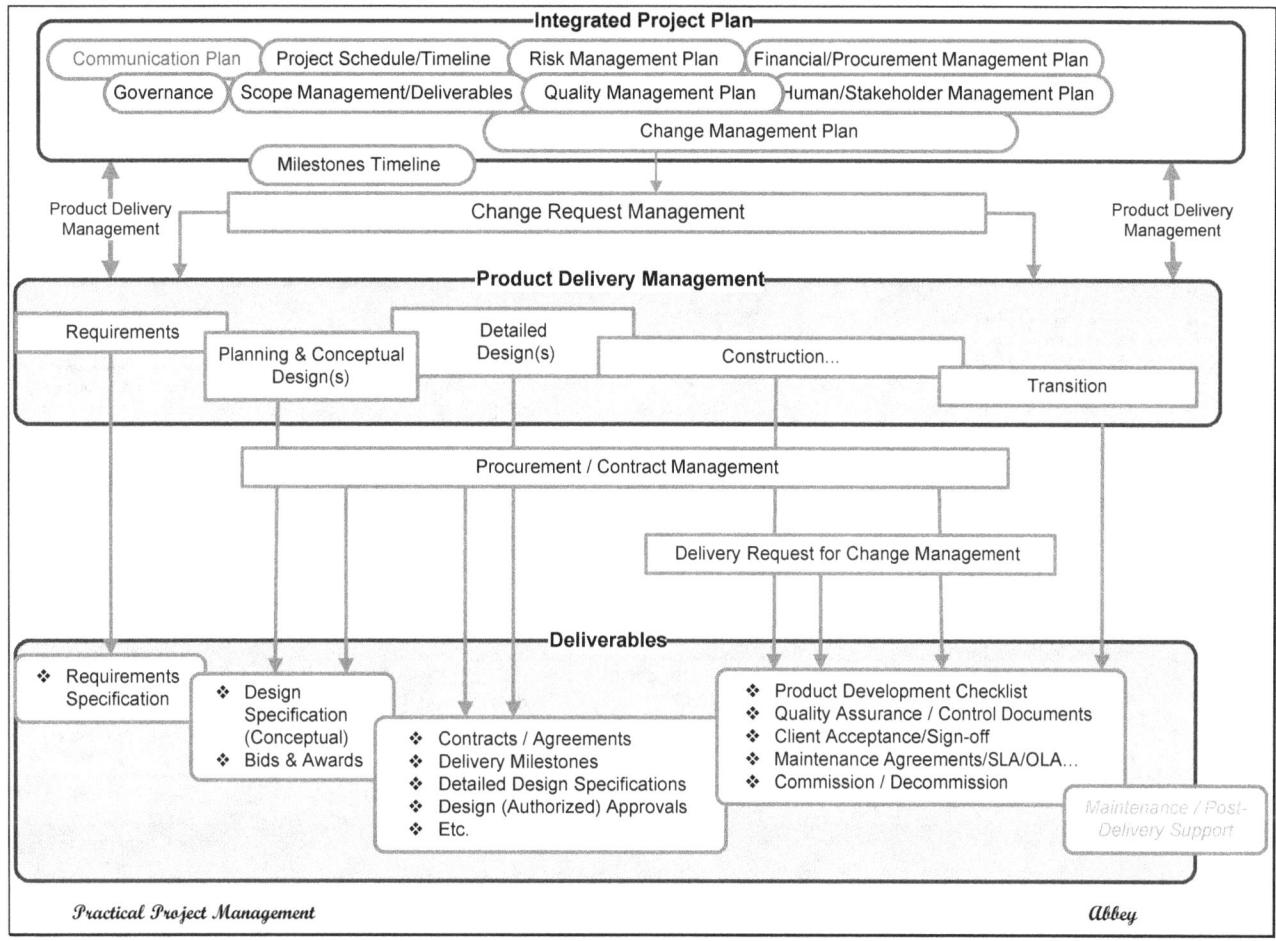

Figure 42 - Deliver Result - Implementation

Quality Assurance

Quality Assurance (QA) includes series of comprehensive testing performed by the product designer, engineers and developers to ensure compliance with regulations, desired quality and overall client requirements, using standard checklist and integrated test plan. Quality assurance may include activities such as laboratory testing, system testing, stress testing and market simulation. Some organizations hire a QA expert to ensure the end-to-end quality of the project management and product delivery management processes and deliverables. A typical QA framework, showing key activities and steps, is shown in Figure 43.

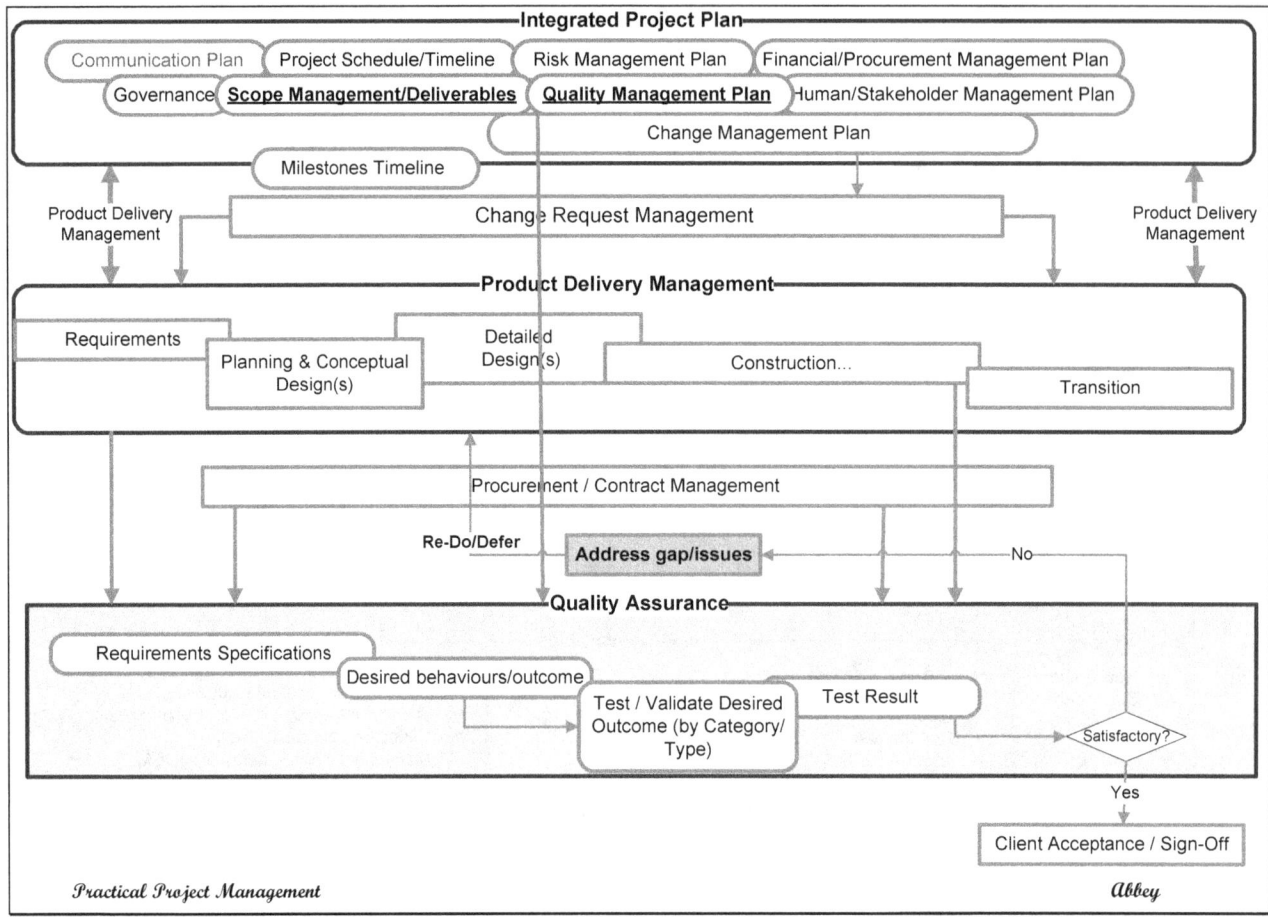

Figure 43 - Deliver Result – Implementation – Quality Assurance

The outcome of the QA determines whether to proceed to user acceptance/sign-off activities or return to the design and/or construction phase in order to resolve and close the identified gaps or issues. Table 17 includes a reference or link to a QA document template.

Table 17 - Quality Assurance Document Template

PPMBook\DeliverResult\PPM_QualityAssurance.doc

Manage Request for Change

This is different from the project scope change management. It involves pre product release change request preparation and management of the approvals of various change controls through the established authorities, internal and/or external to the organization, to ensure safe and unobstructed commissioning (commercialization or production release) of the new product or approved work. This is usually reviewed and approved by the request for change governing body to ensure continuity of operations during and after the commissioning of the new product. Table 18 includes a reference or link to a request for change document template.

Table 18 - Request for Change Document Template

PPMBook\DeliverResult\PPM_RequestForChange.doc

Acceptance/Sign-Offs

This stage includes presentation of the desired outcome (agreed features or functions) to the client, through demonstration, work-through, self testing, quality assurance reports etc. This is to enable the client accept, fully or conditionally, the project outcome or request for compliance. Compliance acceptance is required if there is any issue to be resolved, due to the disparity between the result presented and the agreed client's requirements.

Figure 44 (page 146) shows the client acceptance/sign-off framework, within the context of the product delivery management. The outcome of the client acceptance determines whether to proceed to the commissioning stage or return to the design and/or construction phase in order to resolve and close the identified gaps or issues. Table 19 includes a reference or link to a client acceptance (or contract deliverables sign-off) template.

Table 19 – Client/Product Acceptance Template

PPMBook\DeliverResult\PPM_ProductAcceptance.doc

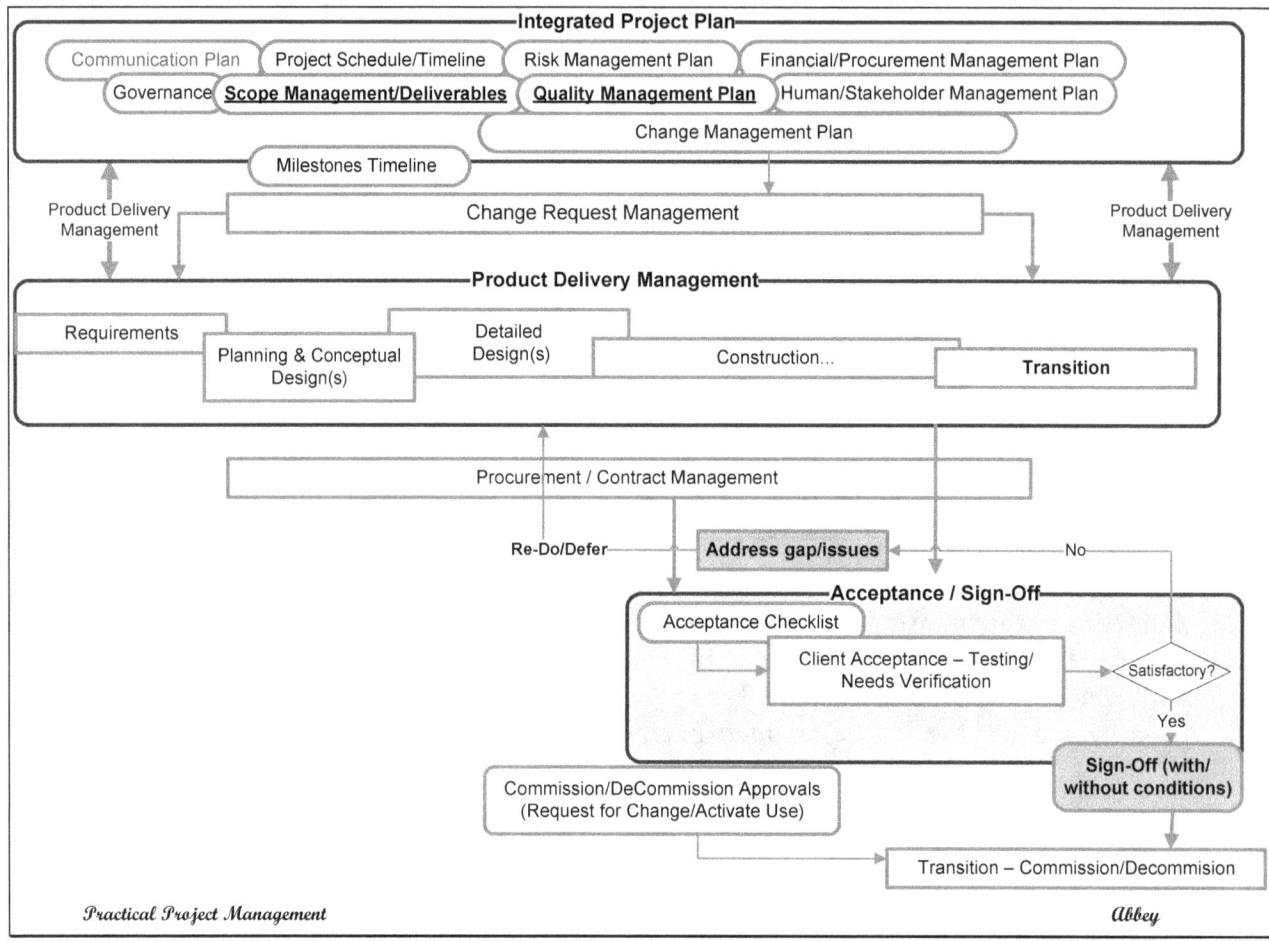

Figure 44 - Deliver Result – Implementation – Acceptance/Sign-Off

Transition

It is important to ensure a smooth transition from the old to the new product or service. A smooth transition could be a major challenge or issue due to lack of accepting responsibility for the successful operations, including maintenance and support, of the new product or service. This could be caused by unwillingness and/or lack of capacity of the service operations and support team in taking up additional support role.

The issue of capacity planning cannot be understated. This could be a real threat to the sustenance of great products and services. Delivering a product without a clear support plan is a major problem to the sustenance of any product or service. This problem has plagued so many great products, leading to a short product life, due to unmanaged breakdown and unhealthy state. Even with a support plan, lack of will to commit to post commissioning support is a major reason why a great product fails to deliver long term value.

It is crucial that as part of the transition, a comprehensive, but simple to use, support guides are provided for ongoing support. Lack of documentation could be a problem to effective operations support of a product or service. Provide knowledge base and reference guides for quick incident and problem resolutions. Engaging the support team during the implementation phase of the project has proved productive in the transition process.

Figure 45 shows the transition framework, including key deliverables.

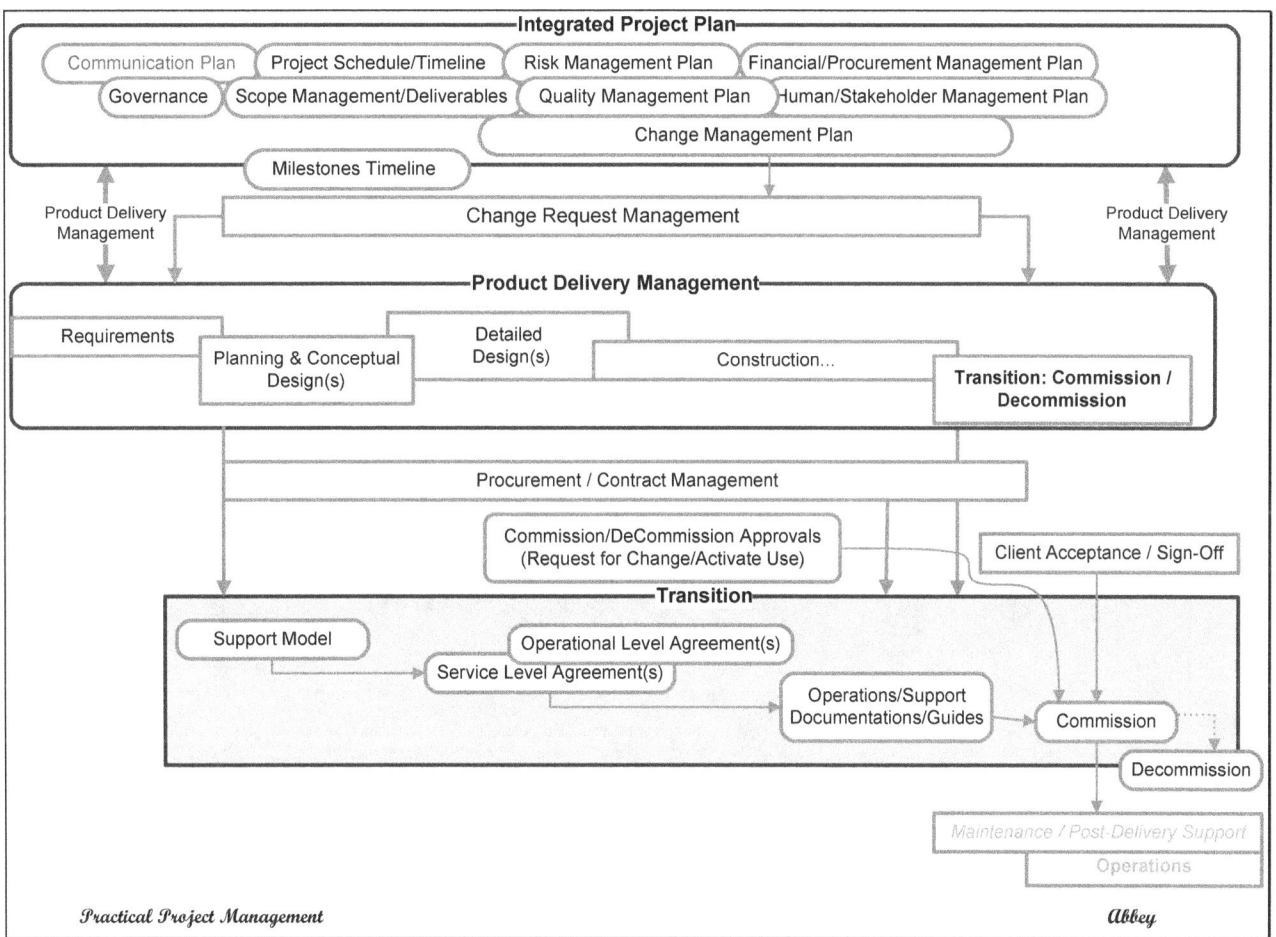

Figure 45 - Deliver Result – Implementation - Transition

In conclusion, in order to make transition effective, the support agreements (service level and operational level agreements) should be formally approved by the relevant stakeholders as commitments to operate the new product or service according to the written agreements.

Chapter 28 - Closing

This is the phase that usually receives the least attention on most projects. Once a project has delivered the desired product(s), most participants want to 'bail out' and move on to another assignment. Figure 46 shows the project closing framework, including activities and deliverables. Communication flows through the closing phase, and there are considerable works that need to be performed to close a project.

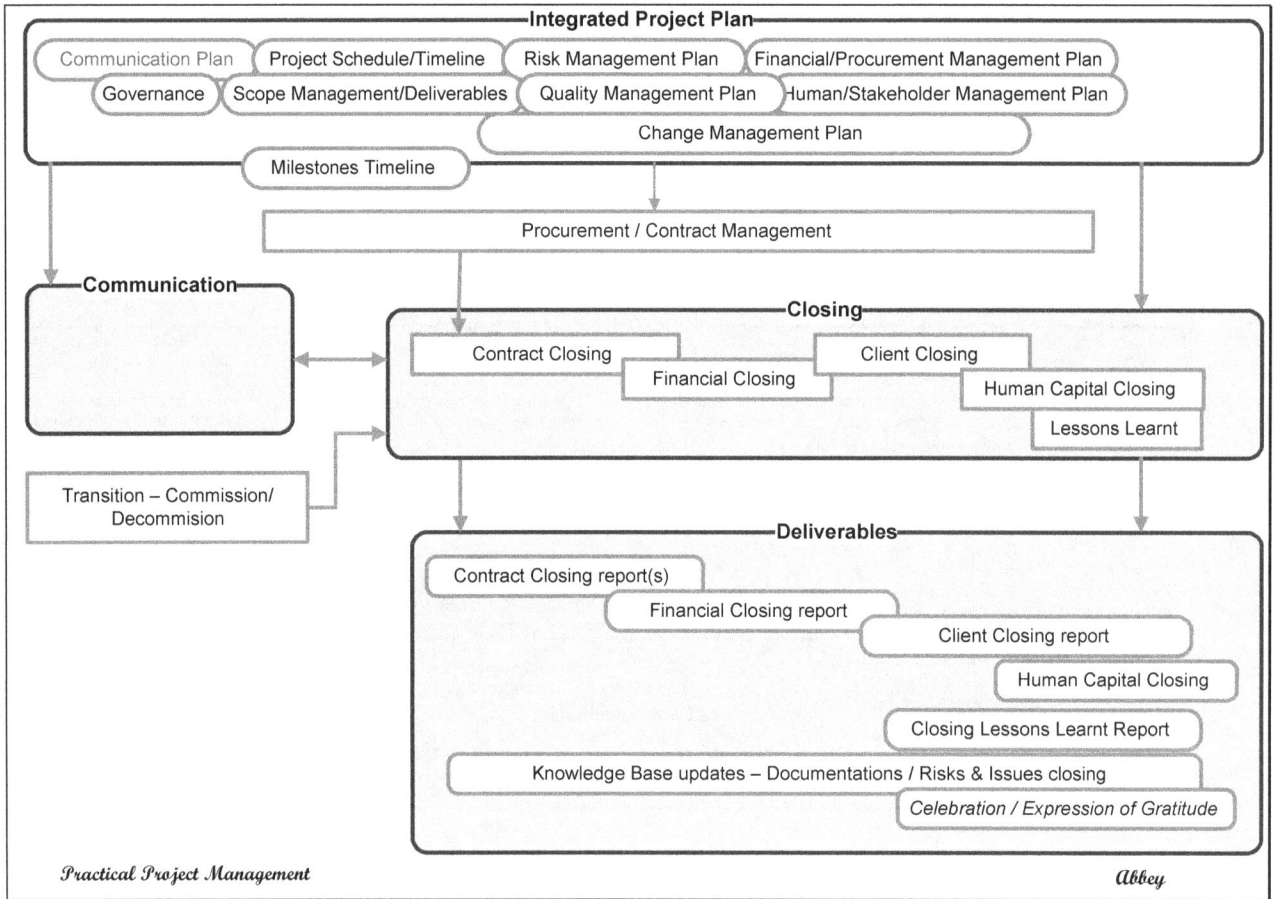

Figure 46 - Deliver Result – Project Closing

Closing Activities and Reports

In order to formally close the project and complete the transition process, the elements that need to be reviewed and reported include the following:

- **Contract closing:** This is the report to bring all the procurement/contract activities to conclusion, by ensuring that all contracts' deliverables are completed and verified. Ensure that payments are made for delivered or completed milestones and all outstanding invoices are paid or scheduled for payment.

- **Financial closing:** This is the overall project financial performance report. It includes contracts, resource, equipment and administration financials indicating plan, actual and variation information.

- **Client closing:** It includes the summary of the overall project performance (desired outcome and actual outcome) in terms of functions, quality, cost and time. The goal of this report is to obtain formal client attestation of satisfaction to the outcome of the project.

- **Lessons learnt:** This is the summary or cumulative of all lessons learnt throughout the project life cycle, including the formal project closing lessons learnt session.

- **Human resource closing:** It includes the report of the project team members' performance and the release of the project human resources.

- **Documentation update:** Normally all project documents are stored in a centrally managed repository, throughout the life cycle of the project. At the project closing, review the project delivery checklist and ensure that all the artefacts are stored in the project document repository, as part of the knowledge base, for future reference.

- **Celebration and expression of gratitude:** It is important to show or express appreciation to all the stakeholders, particularly the project team, that contributed to the success of the project. You could arrange an end of the project get together and/or give out souvenirs (project related gift items and letters of commendations) to commend project stakeholders' contributions.

Table 20 includes references or links to templates for the closing deliverables. You may use or modify them as appropriate.

Table 20 - Closing Documents' Templates

- PPMBook\DeliverResult\PPM_ContractClosing.doc

- PPMBook\DeliverResult\PPM_FinancialClosing.doc

- PPMBook\DeliverResult\PPM_ClientClosing.doc

- PPMBook\DeliverResult\PPM_HRClosing.doc

- PPMBook\DeliverResult\PPM_LessonsLearnt.doc

Chapter 29 - Good Practices

Noises could be distractions, only the wise avoid them in order to sustain their focus.

The following are good practices and quick tips that facilitate the successful delivery of projects. Though some may seem obvious, but they worth emphasizing.

- *Focus* on monitoring milestones, deliverables and work packages' outcomes.

- *Watch for signals* such as schedule slippage, risks and issues. Drill down on causes of deviation and respond with appropriate measure(s) to put the affected activity or event on track.

- *Avoid distraction* due to multi-activities on the project. Ask questions to elicit facts.

- *Keep close contact* with the key stakeholders and be available to provide support as needed.

- *Keep communication simple*, direct and focused.

- *Be diplomatic*, when necessary, but do not misrepresent facts to the stakeholders. The immediate gain could be expensive and jeopardise future opportunities.

- *Show good judgement:* get facts, engage and consult with key stakeholders, before making a decision.

- *Avoid confrontation*, but be direct, be self aware and respectful of others' point of views, even if they appear silly or irrelevant.

- *Avoid panic mode behaviours and events.* Panic does not produce desirable result. You may transfer the same habit to your team members, making a bad situation worse.

- *Be consistent* in your messages and presentations. If there is a change that impacts the original message, make it clear in the latest message. Consistency could be a challenge in situations where facts are manipulated and organization culture of confusing diplomacy with misrepresentation of fact is evident.

- *Make lessons learnt a regular practice.* On most projects, this is an activity that is usually reserved to the end of the project. Make it a habit to identify and record lessons learnt, like you identify and record issues and risks, throughout the project life cycle.

Part 7: Continuous Improvement

This part, the concluding part of this book, is about preventing complacency. It includes the following topics:

- Service Excellence

- Performance Feedback

- Reviews and Lessons Learnt

- Practice Maturity

- Good and Complementary Practices

Blank page

Chapter 30 - Continuous Improvement

"The farther backward you can look the farther forward you can see."   **Winston Churchill**

Continuous improvement of processes, practices, techniques and tools prevent complacency and moves the practitioners and the organization towards maturity and, achieving and sustaining service excellence.

Though this section may be more applicable to service management, its usefulness to effective project management and product delivery management cannot be understated. Its application is relevant to lessons learnt and project knowledge base for maturing the project delivery management and to accomplish service excellence. Service excellence is achievable through these key steps: define, develop, measure, control and improve. These key steps are applicable to quality improvement during the life cycle of a project.

Service Excellence

Service excellence creates the mindset for continuous improvement, believing that things could be done better. Figure 47 shows a service excellence model or framework, including the key steps to building and sustaining service excellence.

A critical success factor or way to establish and sustain competitive advantage is service excellence. Service excellence enables the sustenance and quality of existing products, retains customers and, increases value and returns on investment. Service excellence is not about an after-thought customer service, but a complete sense of service throughout the product or service life cycle.

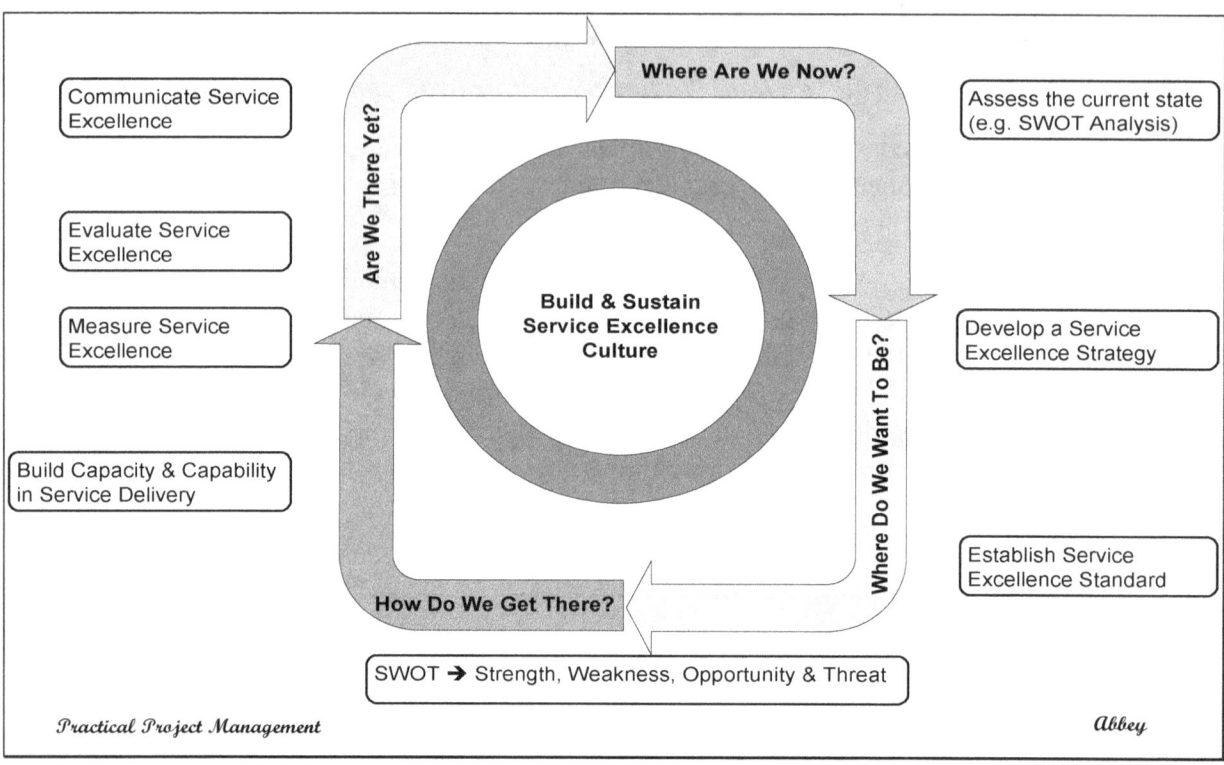

Figure 47 - Service Excellence Model

Performance Feedback

"The key to self-improvement is accurate and honest self-assessment."[6]

Feedback should be sought at every stage in the product or service life cycle, through lessons learnt, good practices and customer survey. Feedback provides vital information to strategy, portfolio and project delivery management. A learning organization values and pays attention to valid and honest feedback. A learning organization is a performing organization. You cannot establish and sustain competitive advantage by counting on luck or guess work. Most business catastrophes are preventable if feedback and warning signals are not ignored.

Figure 48 shows the feedback information flow between various levels of activity domains within an enterprise. Feedback flow is multi-dimensional, that is every point in the value chain provides useful information to fine tune each other's response to emerging issues and changing environment landscape.

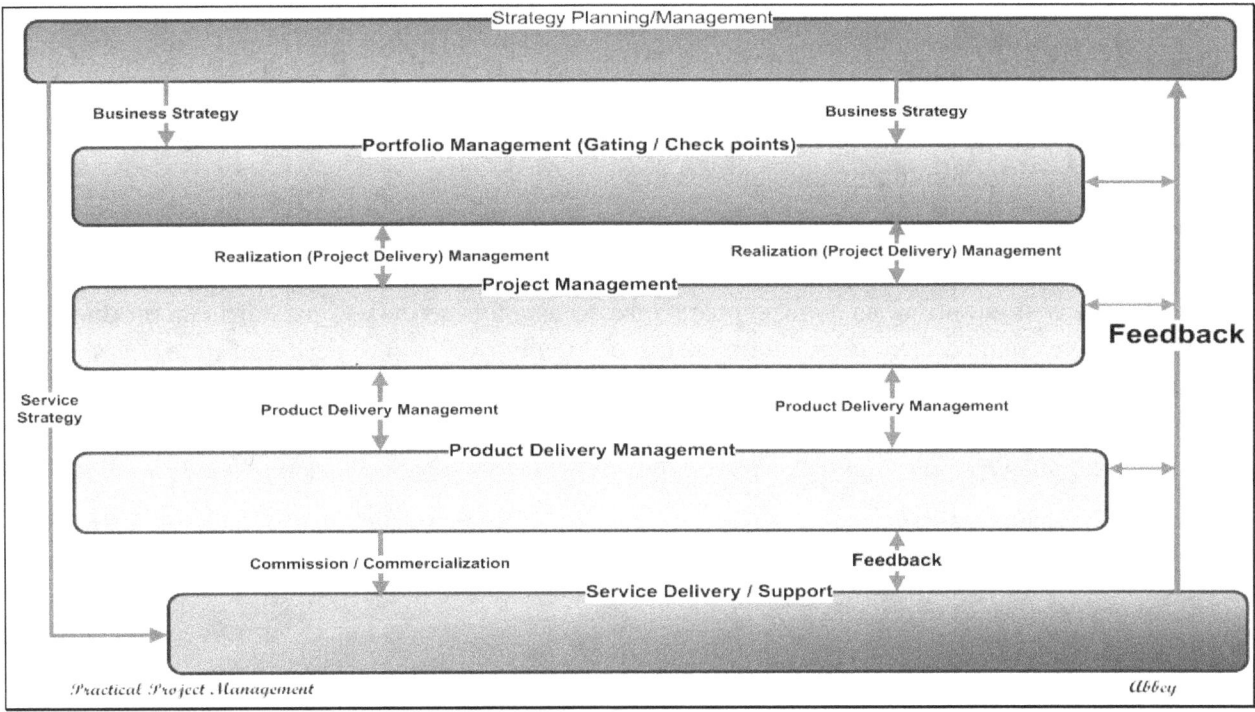

Figure 48 - Performance Feedback

Reviews and Lessons Learnt

"An organization's ability to learn, and translate that learning into action rapidly, is the ultimate competitive advantage."   *Jack Welch*

The world experience cycles of failures, mainly because some people hardly learn from experience. There is hardly any failure that is (entirely) new or not a re-occurrence of the past failure. Mediocrity has contributed significantly to the cycles of failures, which are preventable. For instance, the real-estate bubbles and economic disasters are all cycles of failures, which are preventable by man's actions. This, of course, is debatable, but the central theme and importance of lessons learnt, in project delivery management, cannot be understated.

Naturally, lessons learnt should be part of every project management phase or process group. It should not be reserved till the end of the project or event. Keeping it to the end, could cause you to forget important lessons that occurred during the project life cycle. Doing it during the project life cycle enables you to keep track of all lessons and minimize the effort and time spent on the project closing phase lessons learnt activities. One of the reasons some project stakeholders are not committed to lessons learnt is because most lessons are never considered or acted upon. Not many people want to spend time on things that no one wants or makes use of.

Few wise organizations survive all or most turbulence not because they do not feel the pinch, due to other exogenous shocks beyond their control, but because they have enough buffers and capabilities to weather the storms. Lessons learnt enhance the resilience of a prepared and learning organization to stay above the water.

The ability to learn is part of continuous quality improvement, which has played a major role in sustaining an organization's competitive advantage. Example: the Japanese firms utilized total quality (or continuous quality improvement) as a tool to deliver masterpiece products, which have enabled them to maintain customer loyalty over a long period of time. Lessons learnt provide key inputs to ensure the successful delivery of new and enhanced products or services.

Chapter 31 - Maturity Practice

Maturity is attained through the stakeholders' commitment and consistent use of practical processes, select tools and, most importantly, good and complementary practices. You may talk about maturity levels all the time, without good and complementary practices, they will remain illusive to you. Good and complementary practices, over time, translate into maturity and service excellence.

Project management maturity is the catalyst and nutrient for program and portfolio management maturity. It could also complement the organization strategy by providing lessons learnt opportunities on what worked well and what could be improved upon.

Complementary practices require all stakeholders to understand the importance of key expectations and their implications. It is not good enough to produce a key deliverable (for example, executive report) without a clear use for it and clear feedback on its use and effect, which could aid continuous improvement.

Maturity is not just about compliance with industry methodologies or frameworks. It is about realistic management and governance - that is, being responsible and accountable - and effective and consistent application of processes, techniques and tools that maximize value for an organization or a specific endeavour.

There is no point asking people to do things that cannot be linked to any value creation, just doing anything is not maturity. It has to be what the person or team is committed to do and capable of doing. For instance, asking a sponsor to approve a detailed project schedule, instead of the milestones timeline, which is a summarized version of the schedule, could be unrealistic.

Figure 49, a maturity practice framework, shows the interactions between the maturity domains, approach and complementary practices. The complementary practices and the approach facilitate maturity practices across the maturity domains (portfolio, project, product delivery and service delivery/support management).

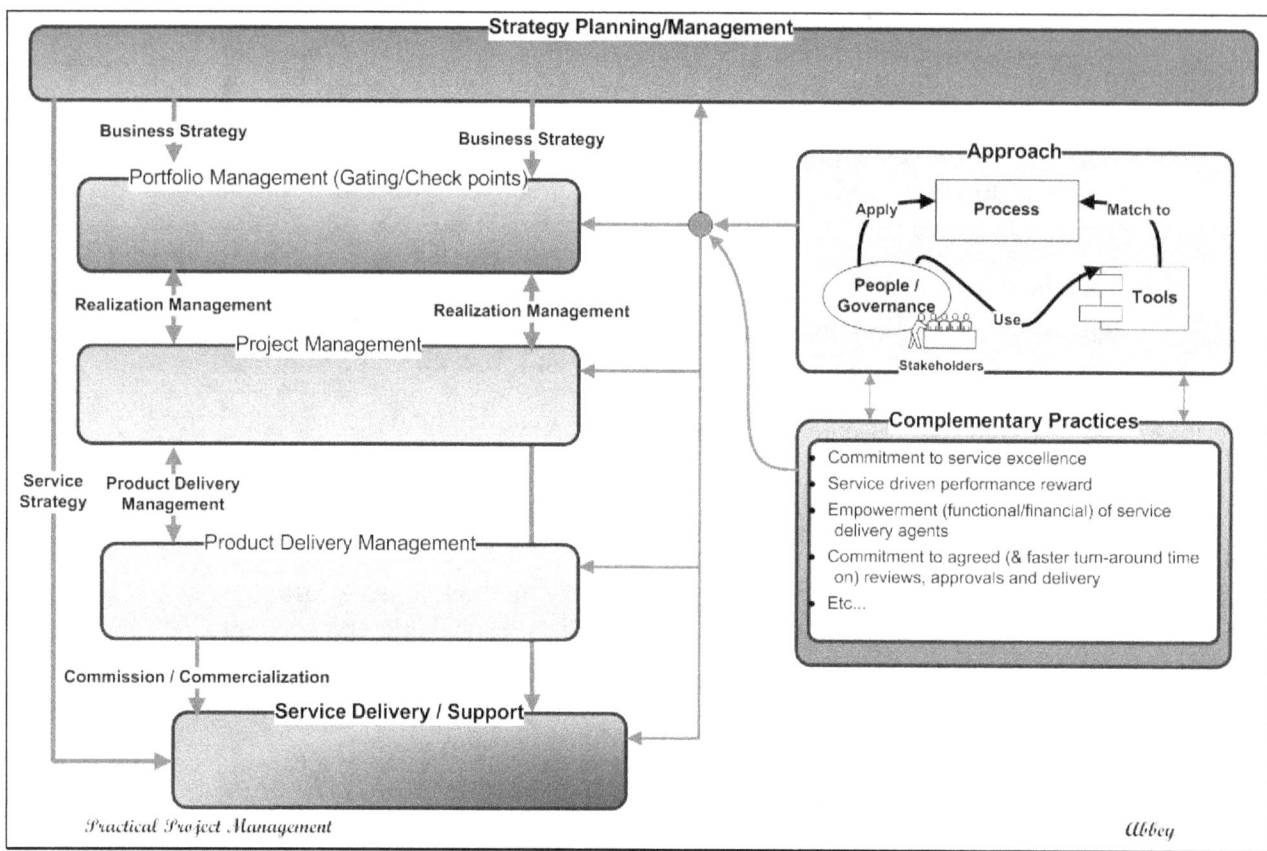

Figure 49 - Maturity Practice

Chapter 32 – Good and Complementary Practices

We have been discussing good practices, all along. Now the focus is on complementary practices, because we are working in a connected world and organization.

- You may not have control over other organizations, departments or legal entities' practices. However, **sharing your practices** with them and demanding their support could encourage and move them to practices that complement your practices.

- **Extend your project governance** or interface to other dependent projects' or units' governance. For instance, making them part of your steering committee or create an interface steering committee.

- **Know your priority:** Focus on top three priorities or deliverables at a time, without loosing sight of other important work activities and deliverables. It is important to keep an eye on the project schedule, particularly on the critical path activities and deliverables.

- **Stay focussed on deliverables and outcome:** Do not be distracted by the work hard habit of jumping from one activity to another, without thinking through what value the activity creates or how it adds value to help you achieve your goals.

- **Spend quality time in planning** every event or activity. Take time to reflect, no matter how short. Engage the project team and other stakeholders, timely and appropriately, in the planning process.

- **Send regular reports,** as agreed in your communication plan or based on ad-hoc request, to your stakeholder groups (project team, sponsor, steering committee etc.).

- **Focus your project team meetings on status review and issues management**. Create other time to 'troubleshoot or workshop' issues. Make use of focus groups to resolve major issues and problems.

- **Team building:** provides great value to promoting team spirit and collaboration among stakeholders and cross-teams.

- **Practice work sharing.** Work sharing enables team members to backup each other. Encourage it and demonstrates the complementary value to the team.

"If A equals success, then the formula is A=X+Y+Z, where X is 'work', Y is 'play', and Z is 'keep your mouth shut'."
                                                                    Albert Einstein.

Blank page

Bibliography

1. Scott, A. (Professor) (2003). *Strategic Planning – Edinburgh Business School.* Pearson Education.

2. Kennedy, G (Professor) (2002). *Negotiation – Edinburgh Business School.* Pearson Education.

3. Covey, S. R. (1989). *Seven Habits Of Highly Effective People.* Simon & Schuster .

4. Financial Times. (2000). *Mastering Strategy – The Complete MBA Companion in Strategy, Financial Times Mastering.* Pearson Education Limited.

5. ISACA. *Control OBjective for Information and related Technology (COBIT).* ISACA.

6. Johnson, C. R. (1998). *CEO Logic – How to Think and Act Like a Chief Executive.* Career Press.

7. Mullins, John W.; Jr., Orville C. Walker; Jr., Harper W. Boyd (2003). *Marketing – Edinburgh Business School.* Pearson Education.

8. Project Management Institute (PMI). (2008). *Project Management Body of Knowledge (PMBOK®).* PMI.

Glossary - Definitions and Descriptions

Strategy: Strategy is the outcome of, or decision based on, the match between the organization distinctive and reproducible competencies, and external environmental factors.

Distinctive competencies cannot be copied or they take longer time to copy. Examples include value chain connection, team culture and copyright innovations.

Reproducible competencies can easily be copied, but still vital to the organization growth and survival. Examples include support services like HR, Finance and Information Technology.

Strategy should be flexible, not static, and adaptable to emerging internal and external factors. Combinations of economic/business techniques and tools are applied to develop and make informed strategic choices on how to take advantage of the organization's strength and environmental opportunities, and respond to weaknesses and threats.

Steering Committee: This is a group of leaders, senior professionals, managers, executives, and sponsors within, and sometimes outside, the organization, who provide the means, help resolve escalated issues and risks, and provide clear path or green field to ensure the success of the project.

Product: This is tangible item designed, developed and delivered to meet the client's needs. In this book the term product is used to denote goods and services. Product and service are sometimes used interchangeably when the intended purpose of a product is to deliver customer service or whereby the product itself is a form of service.

Project: Project is a unique or specific endeavour, with specific start and end dates, undertaken to create a product or service which deliver certain benefits or added value. Project contains set of activities, which utilize resources (people, money and materials) to deliver project goals.

Project management: Project management is the discipline of planning, organizing and managing resources to successfully deliver specific project goals.

WBS - work breakdown structure: WBS represents a project as manageable work packages, which help to define the scope of work for the project. These set of work packages are required to deliver the project goals. Each work package can be used to prepare a statement of work as a contract specification. It is not the same as project schedule. It provides the inputs required to develop the project schedule. To develop an effective WBS you should always have the outcome in mind and ensure that the work required to deliver that outcome are clearly identified and captured as part of the WBS tree structure.

Project schedule: WBS provides inputs required to develop a project schedule, which is the clear articulation of activities, tasks, associated effort and duration, dependencies and resource assignment to complete the work packages and deliverables, and achieve the project goals.

Scope: is the total work, agreed with the client, required to complete a project. It contains set of required products and their associated features or requirements.

Scope management plan: describes how the project scope will be defined, managed, controlled, verified and communicated to the project team and stakeholders. Effective scope management helps to control scope creep.

Term of reference (TOR): sets the direction for undertaking a project. It defines the overall project agenda and desired outcome, how scope will be defined, developed and verified. For small projects, TOR could suffice for project charter. TOR usually includes the vision, objectives, scope and deliverables, funding/budget, timeline and stakeholders. It is prepared after the business case has been approved.

Project-Program management: manages set of related or interdependent projects, which are required to collectively deliver the organization or program goals, which could not be achieved otherwise.

Project-Portfolio management: this is the analysis and administration of groups of existing and new projects and other business activities to deliver strategic organization goals and objectives. The main objective of project portfolio management is to ensure an optimal selection of projects, which maximize value for the organization, stakeholders and/or shareholders.

Operations: include the day-to-day activities or events performed to sustain the organization service. Examples include: customer service desk resolving customer problems, providing after sales support (returns and technical services), road maintenance etc.

Basic investment (financial) evaluation methods:

NPV - net present value: also called time value of money is used to evaluate or appraise a project value creation. It is the total present value of future cash flow over a time period. It is affected by the discount rate or risk-base interest rate.

NPV = Summation of $C_t/(1+r)^t$, where t = time of the cash flow; r = discount rate or rate of return (of a similar market investment/opportunity with the same risk); C_t = net cash flow (inflow - outflow) at time t.

Usually a project with NPV > 0 is preferred for consideration. NPV<0 (loss) and NPV=0 (break even) are not considered, *ceteris paribus (i.e. with other factors remaining the same)*.

IRR - internal rate of return is what the organization used to determine the efficiency of an investment and determines if an investment is worthwhile. It is usually compared to the risk-base market interest rate to make an investment decision. A preferred investment will have IRR > market cost of capital or hurdle rate.

ROI - Return on Investment or rate of return: is usually expressed in percentage per annum, is the ratio of money gain/loss to the amount of investment. It is usually with a risk factor built in. The risk adjusted rate of return on capital invested should be greater than the cost of capital, in order for it to be considered a worthwhile investment.

Note: For NPV and ROI measurements, consistency of the relevant components that make up the composition of these values is very important - details is beyond the scope of this book.

Payback period: is the period of time (usually in years) that it takes for returns on investment to repay the initial cost of investment. Some are measured in raw term while some are measured in present value term. The latter is the preferred method, considering the time value of money. It is measured by time is takes to recover the initial investment.

Cost of borrowing or capital (interest rate): is the expected rate of return the capital provider (or lender) expects to earn on the investment or loan to the business.

Note: A combination of NPV, IRR and payback period (among other considerations such as social, political and environmental factors) is used to make investment financial decision.

Principal-agent: This is the conflict of interests between the principal (employer) and the agent (employee). Principal-agent problem occurs when the agent is acting on his/her own interests which are in conflict with the principal's interests.

Index